Deborah Gallant worked for fifteen years in the radio business as an award-winning on-air newscaster, marketing director, and salesperson. After earning an MBA from the Columbia University Graduate School of Business, she went to work for the ABC Radio Networks, where she caught the Internet bug in 1995. Since then, she has been a manager at a number of Internet firms, including Advance Publications Internet, FamilyPoint.com, a family community start-up, and iVillage.com, the Women's Network. She is currently Senior Vice President of Business Development for Intro Inc., which provides consulting and human resources services to Internet companies.

After earning her MA in English, **Cindy Grogan** joined the radio business as a writer of syndicated programming. She has worked at ABC Radio Networks/New York and AME Radio Networks/Los Angeles, where she first became intrigued by the possibilities of merging the Internet and broadcast, and developed one of the first sites for syndicated radio. Cindy has created original content for a number of Web sites, and is currently a successful freelance writer specializing in broadcast and new media.

Internet Jobs for the Rest of Us

They're Not Just for Geeks Anymore

Deborah Gallant
and Cindy Grogan

BERKLEY BOOKS, NEW YORK

A Berkley Book
Published by The Berkley Publishing Group
A division of Penguin Putnam Inc.
375 Hudson Street
New York, New York 10014

Copyright © 2001 by Deborah Gallant and Cindy Grogan
Cover design by Pyrographx
Text design by Tiffany Kukec

PRINTING HISTORY
Berkley trade paperback edition / March 2001

The Penguin Putnam Inc. World Wide Web site address is
http://www.penguinputnam.com

Library of Congress Cataloging-in-Publication Data

Gallant, Deborah.
Internet jobs for the rest of us : they're not just for geeks anymore / Deborah Gallant
and Cindy Grogan.—Berkley trade paperback ed.
p. cm.
ISBN 0-425-17831-5
1. Telecommunication—Vocational guidance. 2. Internet—Vocational guidance. I.
Grogan, Cindy. II. Title.

TK5102.6 .G35 2001
004.67'8'02373—dc21
00-050791

PRINTED IN THE UNITED STATES OF AMERICA

10 9 8 7 6 5 4 3 2 1

CONTENTS

ACKNOWLEDGMENTS

Deborah would like to offer special thanks to her always supportive husband, Jon, and her (usually) encouraging daughter, Amy. She'd also like to thank her co-author Cindy for helping get this all down on paper!

Cindy would like to thank her late parents, Leslie and Alice, for their unwavering support of her writing career, her sisters, Linda and Leslie, and stepfather, Jimmy Palumbo, for their continuing encouragement. She also thanks Deborah for the brainstorm that led to this book, and for all the soup!

We would like to thank the many people we spoke to in the course of researching this book, whose names were purposely disguised or left anonymous at both their request and the discretion of the authors. No particular individual referred to should be presumed to be any particular actual individual, and any such assumption would be unwarranted.

The authors would also like to offer special thanks to Lisa Swayne of The Swayne Agency, Lisa Considine and Bret Witter of Penguin Putnam, Amy Harcourt of Definitive Marketing, Richard Laermer of RLM Public Relations, Susan Mernit, Stuart Schauman, Madhavi Saifee, Vince Beese, David Ellyatt, Pepper Evans, Allison Tucker, Peter Mazurcyzk of Fusion Design, Joanne Hickson of Fusion Design, Sunny Bates of Sunny Bates Associates, Robert Grass, Kathy Windsor, Franco Moscardi, Michael Wechsler, Gehan Talwatte, Cara Erickson of Bishop Partners, Margaret Haas, Neil Whitley, Michael Keriakos, Marilyn Byrd (for her barbeque sandwich), Duke McKenzie and Donna Introcaso of Intro Inc.

Internet Jobs for the Rest of Us

INTRODUCTION

The Internet Business: Is It for You?

You've heard the story: Some twenty-three-year-old makes a bundle after selling an Internet company he'd started out of his bedroom. Galling, isn't it? Yet the good news is that, as the Internet grows, those little start-ups are moving from the bedroom or garage to offices uptown, faster than you can say "You've got mail!"—and they need regular business people like *you* to help grow them.

To prove it, here are some statistics that should get your attention:

- The Commerce Department estimates that *nearly half* of American workers will be employed in Internet-related jobs by 2006.[1]

- A University of Texas study estimates that in 1998 alone, the Internet was responsible for *1.2 million jobs.*[2]

- Employment in New York City's Silicon Alley alone doubled in just *two years!*[3]

1. Steven K. Paulson, "Gore: Internet Technology Key to Economic Future," Associated Press, June 23, 1999.
2. Stacey Lawrence, "Internet Economy," *Iconocast*, November 11, 1999.
3. http://www.vaultreports.com.

And here all you thought the Internet was good for was ordering holiday hams or sending jokes through e-mail. **Newsflash:** *It's the biggest career opportunity in decades.*

Joining the Internet business has several payoffs:

- Despite some turbulence, it's one of *the* growth industries of the twenty-first century.

- Money. It's a gold rush out there and you can quite possibly reap both long- and short-term financial rewards. Just imagine the value of the stock options handed out at AOL, Yahoo, or Amazon.com to those who were there at the beginning. On second thought, don't—it's too painful!

- Because the Internet is a brand-new world, creativity and new ideas—no matter how nutty they seem—are welcome. Plus, the Internet business offers a fast-paced work environment that's never boring!

Okay, so you think that most of the people working in the Internet industry wear pocket protectors and are what we affectionately call "geeks." True, the techies—those who build the hot Web sites or newest "application"—are the ones you mostly hear about on CNN, but as the Internet continues to grow at an explosive rate, it needs the same specialists as any successful company. Thus people who do "real" jobs, from sales and accounting to design and marketing, are finding a brand-new niche in the Internet industry.

If you have this nagging feeling that you've somehow missed the boat on the Web revolution, get that notion out of your head right now. As Michael Parsons writes in *The Industry Standard,* one of the Internet's top business publications, "Every CEO I speak with says that hiring is the No. 1 item on the agenda; there simply aren't enough skilled people around, and you can't have sales with a sales director, a marketing plan without a marketing director."[4]

But while there's definitely plenty of room for you at the party, the timing factor *does* count for something in the corporate culture of the Internet. There are people who've been doing this for a few years, the early believers. To them, those just joining the game aren't as cool. Do yourself a huge favor by staying humble with this crowd until you learn the ropes. Ignore any attitude or chips on the shoulder (they do exist) and learn from their experience. Once they see that you're as enthusiastic as they are, the lines between the early and the late arrivals will blur.

You may have the idea that the Internet industry is populated exclusively by the latté-sipping, black-clad, under-thirties crowd—and that you don't fit in. Scratch that thought. Although it *is* a hotbed for young, creative types, Internet firms (and their venture capital partners) need people who've got some mileage on their résumé. We can't emphasize it enough: *There's room for you.* In fact, many young Net entrepreneurs actively seek out seasoned professionals, because no matter how excruciatingly hip the office may be, at the end of the day it's still a business. In fact, you might be surprised to know that a recent survey indicates that 38 percent of new media employees are between thirty and forty years old, and 29 percent are over forty.[5]

Two other points are worth mentioning here: If you're a woman, you'll find that, while the Internet business *is* male dominated, there's far more opportunity for you to soar than in the traditional workplace. And if—male or female—you're concerned about whether you may be too old for the Internet game, hear

---

4. Michael Parsons, "When Money's No Object," *The Industry Standard*, February 7, 2000, p. 13.

5. "Industry Profile: New Media," *Alley Cat News*, April 2000, p. 20.

this: The truth is that an adventurous spirit and a youthful attitude are what really count—not your age.

How do we know all this? Because we've experienced it firsthand, making the switch from working in large, established corporations to a world where every day is casual Friday and a shocking number of people bring their dogs to the office! Traditional corporate life *did* have its advantages: nice offices, good benefits, and a prestigious company name on your résumé. However, we were both frustrated that our creative ideas were often dismissed because of budgets, office politics, and stodgy corporate goals (the bathroom was also too far away, but that's another story).

When it came to salary and promotions, we could expect to go only so far, only so fast. So we jumped feet first into the Internet game. Deborah has worked in the Internet departments of buttoned-down brick-and-mortar companies and also at wild-and-crazy dot-com start-ups. She's hired, fired, recruited, managed, and consulted in the Web world—in short, she's *lived* everything we'll be covering in this book.

Cindy opted to leave the nine-to-five world and go freelance, finding a new home for her writing skills in the digital world. She's definitely *not* the tech type, but has learned to embrace Internet technology and new media, carving out a satisfying, cre-

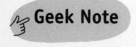 **Geek Note** What about education? At this point, having some experience in the Internet industry is generally more important than having an MBA. But having that degree never hurts, and if you're going to work for a start-up firm with a less-road-tested staff, a degree could give you an edge.

ative, and lucrative career niche. And she'll tell you that the transition was less aggravating than learning to drive a stick shift or making flan.

The point? *We* successfully reconfigured already established careers to join the Internet business—and so can *you*.

Okay, so exactly *how* do you, a top salesperson/accountant/PR person, make the switch? In the following chapters, we'll provide a road map, showing you *exactly* how to transfer your present job from Point A (the traditional work world) to Point B (the Internet business world). Besides detailed profiles of various Internet job opportunities (and there are a lot of 'em), we'll share "insider tips" to make your entry into the Web world a bit smoother.

We should mention, however, that just like pro wrestling, opera, or pickled herring, the Internet industry isn't for everyone. It's booming alright, but with that boom comes plenty of chaos, long hours, less job security, and working conditions that Mr.-Corner-Office-with-a-Window may not exactly thrive in. In fact, we'd be remiss if we didn't mention that the volatility, excitement, and unpredictability of the Internet world is leading some who've taken the plunge to climb out of the pool and head back to corporate life. The dot-com life simply wasn't for them.

Before you go rushing into your boss's office with a letter of

 **Author's Note** We talked with dozens and dozens of people to get this information, and found that we got the best insights, the real deal, when we talked "off the record" (the extra round of Cosmopolitans didn't hurt either). The trade-off was agreeing to keep our sources largely anonymous. In some instances, we've changed a name or created a composite of several individuals' experiences. Think of it as our version of the Witness Protection Program.

resignation, first take our quiz to find out how well you're suited to life online.

Are You the Internet Type?

Pick the answer that best describes you:

1. As a kid, you were happiest with:

   A. Coloring books
   B. Blowing up GI Joes in the backyard
   C. Fingerpaints

2. You're being offered a fantastic new job, but the workplace is less than ideal. The offices are tiny and dark, the copier keeps breaking down, and a family of roaches lives near the coffee machine. You:

   A. Start thinking that your old job really isn't that bad after all
   B. Bring in a couple of plants for your office, a can of Raid, and locate the nearest Starbucks
   C. Figure you can spearhead a corporate redecorating campaign

3. After successfully completing a big project, your boss calls you in. You're expecting a big "attaboy/girl" and a raise—instead, you get a pink slip. How do you react?

   A. Panic and head to the nearest bar to trash the Corporate Weasels responsible for this decision

B. Panic for five minutes, then start brainstorming on your next gig

C. Panic, then start planning a vacation with part of your severance pay before you even think about your next job

4. Back when you did homework, under what conditions did you work best?

A. With ear plugs
B. With Black Sabbath on the stereo, cranked to "11"
C. With a plate of Oreos and lite jazz music in the background

5. Which *Gilligan's Island* castaway do you most identify with?

A. Mr. Howell
B. The Professor
C. Gilligan

SCORING

If You Picked Mostly A's: You like structure, routine, and security—qualities that Ford may be known for, but not the Internet industry. It may be a little too wild and woolly for someone who's as comfy in a suit as you are. Go ahead and investigate the Internet opportunities we'll outline, but use extra care if you opt to make the switch.

If You Picked Mostly B's: You're resourceful, hardy, and flexible enough to ride the roller-coaster that is the Internet world. Less-than-ideal work conditions, unpredictable hours, and a little anxiety don't throw you—in fact, they may inspire your best work. Welcome aboard!

If You Picked Mostly C's: A definite . . . "maybe." Although you're not as by-the-book as a four-star general, you're not as comfortable with change as, say, a drag queen. The Internet world may suit you, but target companies that have achieved some stability as your professional home.

Now What?

Okay, now that you know whether or not you might click with Internet business, let's get down to brass tacks. As we mentioned, we'll provide a snapshot of how your present career works in the Internet world. Even though we know you're probably tempted to flip ahead to "your" chapter and gloss over the rest, we strongly urge you to read this book cover to cover. There are useful tidbits scattered throughout, and the more you know about the whole Internet business picture, the more successful you'll ultimately be.

In upcoming chapters, you'll also learn the buzzwords to help you talk the talk, how the hiring process works (guess what? a great résumé and a power suit won't cut it) and how to get a piece of the financial action.

Of course, if you're tempted to move your skills into cyberspace but walking away from a familiar work environment is just not an option, there *is* a middle ground, working on the Internet development side of a traditional company, maybe even the one that presently employs you. This book can help you there, too.

David or Goliath

One of the first questions you *must* ask yourself is what kind of Internet environment is best for your goals. The industry has matured; it's not just about hotshot start-ups anymore. We've divided Internet firms into two categories (not that it's always that clear-cut, but we had to create some sort of distinction). We'll refer to them as such throughout this book.

Goliaths: Goliath companies have a few years under their belts. Yahoo, Amazon, and AOL are good examples. They have many employees, real offices, and plenty of funding and have ridden out the initial bumps to establish a (they hope) solid future. They certainly aren't immune to acquisitions, mergers, or a dot-com downturn, but the potential fall-out would likely be less intense if any of those things happened (they probably won't fold altogether and you'll have a shot at keeping your job or getting a better one within the new structure). A Goliath firm offers stability and perhaps a closer match to what you presently do; you may find the work environment more familiar, you'll get regular paychecks, and there's an actual administrative staff to help prepare presentations. With all that, however, comes some of the

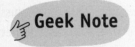 **Geek Note** Plenty of people want to get into Internet business—so it's not surprising that the frenzy is breeding some confusion. In New York's Penn Station, for example, Deborah was handed a flyer promoting an "Internet Business Opportunity," which turned out to be an online pyramid scheme. This is definitely *not* the kind of job we'll be covering, nor will we examine the phenomenon of day trading. Just so we're clear.

same limitations of the place you're leaving behind, such as politics and a more-defined pecking order. The old corporate culture hasn't had as much time to take root at a Goliath Internet firm—but it has taken root nonetheless.

Davids: Davids are the small companies, the start-ups, the ones that live in hopes of being acquired by a Goliath, or at least of nabbing several million more in venture capital until they become hot on their own. The atmosphere is usually more creative—and unpredictable. For example, if you're a salesperson, you probably won't have the luxury of a sales support staff and will have to do much of the legwork yourself. At a David, you may also find your job changing substantially or vanishing altogether in the blink of an eye. However, these companies are often where the real opportunity lies, especially if you have no Net experience. Log some time at a David company, and you may find yourself with some stock options. One thing's a guarantee—you'll walk away with the most important commodity of all: *industry experience.*

Before you make a decision, think seriously about what your tolerance for risk is. It will help you focus your efforts as you read through this book to know whether you're a steady Goliath type or a go-get-'em David.

The Internet business place welcomes people with fresh ideas. It's the perfect arena for people who are unafraid to roll up their sleeves and get the job done, regardless of what title is on their office door (assuming they're lucky enough to *have* an office!). Almost anything is possible—because it's an industry that evolves from day to day. And the potential for you to benefit from all your creativity and hard work is unlimited.

We won't kid you: Making the leap into this new industry can be frustrating, exhausting, and a little scary at times—but keep in mind that no matter how unfamiliar or intimidating this all may seem to you now, it's still *just a job*. Not every day makes headlines on Wall Street; you won't be asked to build a search engine or split the atom your first week. Besides, by the time you finish this book, you'll have a good lay of the Internet landscape and be confident about taking the first step.

As you move into this industry, you'll have the satisfaction of knowing you're part of history in the making . . . and that your talents and abilities are being used to the fullest.

Up for the challenge? Then turn the page—your new career is waiting.

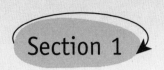

INTERNET BUSINESS 101

Whether it's Twister or the World Cup, if you want to get in the game, you have to know the ground rules. The same goes for the Internet business—and here's where we give 'em to you.

In the next couple of chapters, we'll tell you:

- The different kinds of businesses that are thriving on the Web (not everyone is selling books or auctioning Elvis statuettes).

- The business models supporting the incredible Internet boom. Which ones actually make money? You'll want to know this to make an informed decision about your future.

- The practical skills you'll need. Okay, we promised you this was not a book for or about geeks—but you can't expect to move into a technology industry without some basic tools. Trust us, these skills are painless and simple to learn. Besides, if you don't learn them, you don't stand a chance of landing an Internet job.

- A glossary of Web-speak that will help you sound like you know what you're doing until you actually do.

Let's get started.

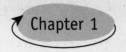

Chapter 1

YOUR INTERNET BUSINESS BRIEFING

Let the Games Begin

First Things First!

We're assuming you have a fundamental understanding of how to get logged on. If not, stop right here and get some grounding: Books on basic Internet skills are great, but the most important thing is to get to a computer and spend some quality time with it. Borrow a friend's, head to the library, or stay late after work. Then just poke around: Visit lots of different sites, play games, participate in chat rooms and message boards, set up an e-mail account and use it.

Try Media Metrix's Web site (http://www.mediametrix.com). As one of the ratings services, it lists the top-rated sites, updated monthly. Visit these popular destinations, and you'll get a good feel for what people are doing on the Internet. It won't be long before you're an old pro. *Then* come back and join us!

A (Mercifully Brief) History of the Internet

Cindy remembers a time not so long ago when she practically had to wrestle her boss to the ground to get him to sign off on developing a Web site for his company. To upper management, it just didn't seem "necessary." Now, any firm without an Internet presence is seen as hopelessly behind the times—and missing out on an important brand-new management tool and revenue source.

Ironically, the Internet was not originally envisioned as the wide-open commercial frontier it's become. It began in 1969 as a sort of "computer co-op" between the Department of Defense and several research universities. Gradually, more universities and military agencies hopped onto the "interconnected network" (hence, "Internet"). By the 1980s, high-speed, long-distance phone lines were being built to connect these supercomputing centers.

Until the early 1990s, commercial traffic was *verboten* on the Internet because the whole enterprise was government funded. But then, the feds changed their minds, opening the door to for-profit Internet service providers—and the unwashed masses (that would be all of us). At the time, it's unlikely they had any notion that the Internet would begin fueling a new economy and rewrite many of the accepted rules of business.

Naturally, this growing commercialization irritated the research types who began referring to the interlopers on their turf as "newbies." It's also opened on-going debates about how much commercialism is okay, the limits of free speech, privacy, and other thorny issues.

Because the Internet began as a free resource, the introduction of for-profit players has not always gone smoothly. Long-time users who suddenly had to pay for information that was once available for nothing has an effect on how they view a site. Businesses find themselves seeking to maintain the delicate balance between the Internet's image as an ultra-democratic place where big companies and big government have yet to dominate—and trying to make a buck.

How Do Internet Businesses Make Money?

When Bill Schrader, PSINet chairman and CEO, was interviewed by *Interactive Week* and asked when his company would stop building and start paying off debts, he answered. "Anybody in my position who would answer that question with a date should be fired."[1] His response gives you a pretty fair assessment of the real answer to our question—which is that most Internet businesses *don't* make money. Of course they fully intend to—someday—and here's a quick overview of how they plan to do it.

E-COMMERCE/TRANSACTION

Many experts think the real upside of the Internet is getting people or businesses to buy stuff online that they ordinarily buy through some other channel. This covers everything from your groceries to booking your vacation to buying a car. In fact, most Internet firms name "transactions" like these as their main revenue stream.[2]

The big companies and brands in this category include Amazon, eToys, Cars Direct, Pets com, and Planet Rx. It's interesting to note that in the earliest days of e-commerce traditional retailers were *not* the Internet e-mail leaders, new brands established strongholds online and started changing buying patterns. However, the old-line retailers have started catching up; and at this point, the race could be anyone's.

An offshoot to be reckoned with in e-commerce is in the business-to-business (B2B) area Companies are using the technology of the Internet to streamline their operations, order supplies, and improve customer service, saving them a bundle in the process. Because of this, experts estimate that B2B sales will

---

1. "CrossTalk," *Interactive Week*, February 7, 2000, p. 90.
2. "Looking for Funding 1999," *AlleyCat News*, December 1999, p 74.

eventually be six times as large as business-to-consumer (B2C) sales.[3]

ADVERTISING-SUPPORTED SITES

Whether it's the Oscars or that hot sitcom, your free entertainment on TV isn't really "free"—it's funded by commercials. The same rule applies on the Web. Most content sites support themselves by selling advertising or sponsorships. This category makes up the second-largest revenue stream on the Internet.[4]

Web advertising typically takes the form of a "banner ad," smaller "tile" or "button" ads, or those annoying pop-ups ("interstitials"). Examples of ad-supported sites include the big portals like Yahoo and Excite, newspapers like the *New York Times*, and special-interest sites such as CBS Sportsline.

SUBSCRIPTIONS/REGISTRATIONS

A lucky few sites have such valuable content that they can charge for it. They're few in number; even Microsoft failed when it initially tried to charge for its online magazine, *Slate*. However, if the content on a site can support a per-user charge, it can become profitable pretty quickly. Online gaming sites and porn sites are two categories that pull this off—and they may be the only ones making any real money. The financial information arena is another (e.g., *The Wall Street Journal*).

INTERNET SERVICE PROVIDERS

Internet service providers (ISPs) are the companies that give individuals and businesses access to the Internet. Some do it over

---

3. Laura Cohn, "B2B: The Hottest Net Bet Yet?" *Business Week*, January 17, 2000, p. 36.
4. "Looking for Funding 1999."

plain old telephone lines, some with the new higher-speed connections like a digital subscriber line (DSL) and some through cable television lines. Many of these players go beyond offering subscribers Internet access for their monthly fee: They create content and communities within their own site to keep their users happy (like AOL). Some ISPs even give away or lease the computer as part of the monthly package (sort of like Gillette giving away razors to get you to buy its blades for the rest of your life). ISPs have a viable business model, and many of them have been making money. That could change however, as a growing number of firms are offering free Internet access. Underlying free access is the hope that enough advertising can be sold to cover their costs, placing these ISPs firmly in the "ad sponsorship" business model.

COMPANIES WITH GOODS AND SERVICES THAT FUEL THE INTERNET ECONOMY

Companies that fuel the Internet economy make up a big category that lumps a lot of different businesses together. With the boom in Internet business, there's an accompanying need for the stuff that makes it all go, like the following.

Hardware: Hardware includes personal computers, components, network routers, servers, and high-speed access lines. Examples include Cisco Systems; Exodus, one of the biggest hosting services; and Intel, which has a virtual monopoly on the chips inside personal computers.

Software: The technology that runs the Internet or specific applications is the software. Examples are Microsoft with its Windows operating system and *Internet Explorer* browser.

B2B Services: These are companies that meet the needs of other companies in Internet space by selling very specialized services. An example is DoubleClick, which creates ads for Web publishers and can sell their ad inventory for them. There are also Internet advertising agencies, like Agency.com, that build banner ads and Web development shops that plan Internet business strategy and build sites. Some of the Goliath players here include Razorfish and MarchFIRST.

Application Service Providers: A rapidly growing subcategory in business services is the application service providers (ASPs), which allow companies to outsource complicated software applications. For example, a firm going into e-commerce can now simply use the ASP's "shopping cart" program, rather than install and maintain an expensive one in-house. ASPs generally make their money by charging licensing fees to their clients.

The Internet has galvanized activity in other branches of the corporate world as well: There are the public relations firms that specialize in Internet publicity, magazines that write only about the Internet economy, and trade shows that cater to the Internet crowd. You'll now find headhunters who recruit exclusively for the Internet, law firms that specialize in new media issues, and accountancies that focus on new media clients. And, of course,

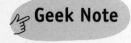 **Geek Note** There's a growing opinion that hardware and software categories are rapidly going the way of the eight-track—and that the future in the technology business is in devices that integrate hardware, software, and service (such as the aforementioned ASPs). Only time will tell how this scenario shakes out.

there are the companies that provide services that keep Internet businesses humming, such as UPS and Federal Express, which deliver all those things ordered online. These particular businesses may not be what you had in mind when you picked up this book—but they *are* hot places to find a job and do require Internet savvy to succeed.

There are two other bonuses to working at these kinds of "fringe" firms:

- Many are actually profitable so there's much more stability. They sell traditional goods and services—but to a specialized market where there's plenty of demand and cash flow.

- They provide another way to get your foot in the door. For instance, an attorney could go to work for a law firm with a new media specialty as his or her first step to becoming in-house counsel at a start-up.

BRICK-AND-MORTAR BUSINESSES WITH INTERNET DEPARTMENTS OR DIVISIONS

The Internet group within a traditional businesses is a great place to get an education in Web fundamentals—without the pressures associated with working at a start-up or giving up years of vesting for your pension. Their business models will generally fit one of those we've already listed; just make sure the company has a clear idea of what it wants to accomplish with its Internet division (more than "just put up a Web page") or you won't learn very much. We'll cover this angle of going dot-com at a not-com in greater detail in chapter 11.

If you thought cyberspace was big before, take a moment to consider what you've just learned—your career opportunities are limitless! And here's one more tantalizing nugget to ponder: Marc

Andreessen, the pioneer who developed the *Netscape* browser, estimates that there will be a *thousand-fold-increase* in the number of Internet companies over the next ten years.[5] Surely there's a place for you!

Exciting stuff, right? However, the cold reality of the Internet's *true* financial state brings us back to that David and Goliath issue we raised earlier. There are Internet companies that actually make money, but there are plenty that don't (yet), that'll dazzle you with lots of talk about the future. We can't stress it enough: This is an entrepreneurial world. You must seriously consider which type of Internet company best matches your goals and tolerance level for risk.

Start-Up Versus Established Internet Firm: Which Is Right for You?

It seems strange to call any firm "established" in the breakaway Internet culture, but (relative) stability has come to many Goliath firms. Stability comes at a price, though. The Goliaths find themselves adopting some—if not all—of the traits of the traditional workplace, including a bureaucracy that can limit your opportunities and slow exciting projects to a crawl. And never get the idea that just because a Goliath has been around for a bit that it's all smooth sailing. One of our sources says that his company still endures near-constant growing pains as it strives to keep the balance sheet healthy and catch up to traditional firms who've had years to smooth out their internal operations systems. Layoffs and re-orgs are not uncommon as they grow. After all, this is still the Internet—even at a Goliath, the pace is still bound to be frantic.

---

5. Gary Arlen, "Andreessen's Power of Ten," http://www.digitrends.com, October 29, 1999.

The pace of work life at a David is qualitatively different—there's literally no time to waste. You're building a company from scratch, hoping to turn it into a success ASAP. With that goal comes insane deadlines and daily worries over funding. Besides actually getting a viable company/product off the ground, a David has the extra fun of courting the venture capital community with all the pressures *that* happy task entails: dog-and-pony shows, endless meetings, and the like.

This uncertainty drives the David company until one of their financing strategies plays out—for better or worse (but in the Internet culture, having been part of a failed company is a badge of honor and doesn't prevent people from successfully jumping to the next opportunity).

Now do an honest gut check: Does the prospect of working at a Goliath make you breathe easier, knowing your move into the Internet world doesn't have to be a bungee jump into the unknown? Or does it make you yawn? Does the David scenario make you break into a cold sweat or does it give you a rush? It's worth some serious soul searching to determine what you ultimately want from your Internet career—and how you'll deal with the inevitable challenges.

By now, you should have a pretty good sense of the range of great career opportunities on the Internet. Let's move on to filling your personal tool kit with the things that will help you get started.

Ever wonder where all these dot-coms are coming from? Here's how many a new venture gets started:

* Someone (usually a young someone) working in the world of technology comes up with a cool new idea. We'll call him Dot-Com Danny. He and a few of his friends either work on the idea at night or quit their jobs to develop a business plan and a prototype. They may use their own money at this stage or beg from friends and relatives (their "angel" investors).

* Danny and Co. launches the product or Web site to gauge early reaction. This is the "beta test," or "soft launch," phase.

* Next, Danny uses every connection he has to get his business plan into the hands of the key venture capitalists (VCs) in Silicon Valley (aka Sand Hill Road) or Silicon Alley (New York). There are investors elsewhere, but the biggest names are in those two places.

* If a VC bites, Danny does his best to keep as much of the company for himself and his partners as possible during the negotiation—and get the infusion of cash he needs to build his business. Danny will eventually need to return for more cash (another round of financing) to keep things going.

* If he successfully secures financing, Danny moves quickly to grab his market niche before someone else does. In just a few weeks, he hires lots of people, rents offices and equipment, then . . .

* . . . he builds, builds, builds! The pace is frantic and caffeine is a constant companion as the team struggles to prove the idea has merit. Danny and his partners are out there making alliances, marketing the heck out of the company, and doing whatever it takes to ensure it gets a toehold in the landscape.

Then it can go as follows:

* The company goes for an initial public offering ("goes IPO"). This is how a few people have gotten really, *really* rich. They hold a substan-

continued . . .

tial percent of the company and, although it may not be worth anything while the company is private, as soon as it's public, those shares
now have a quantifiable (though potentially highly volatile market
value they didn't have before (we'll cover the equity issue in chapter
15).

or

* Danny sells his company to another player or combines it with one in
a similar space. This scenario is far less painful than dealing with an
IPO and public markets, but it may lack that killer payoff. Hotmail sold
itself to Microsoft this way.

or

* The good idea isn't really that good—there's too much competition or
Danny just can't pull it off. In any case, after a few rounds, the VCs
don't want to invest anymore, no one wants to buy the company, and
Danny throws in the towel. VCs don't like to see their investments end
up this way, so they do anything they can to make sure it doesn't
happen. But sometimes it does. One travel-related site we know of
(that shall remain anonymous) established its business model in a
world in which airlines paid a $30 commission on every plane ticket
sold. However, by the time the site got off the ground (no pun intended), the prevailing model had drastically changed—average commissions had dropped to $10. The site couldn't react fast enough to
this major change. The backers eventually sold it to a consortium of
companies—and not one employee saw a dime in stock options.

 **Geek Note** There are two interesting business trends within the Internet. One is *incubators,* in which a well-funded company (or individual venture capitalist) works with several start-ups, offering business guidance, cheap office space, and day-to-day support like managing payroll in exchange for a piece of the company. The idea is that the support will help speed up the process for that start-up to go public.

The other trend is Internet *holding companies,* which springs from a Japanese concept called *kieretsu.* Basically, these groups of companies prosper under a single umbrella. CMGI is one such Internet umbrella; IdeaLab is another. The individual firms may exist in different locations and do different things, but they rely on resources and business support from both the parent firm and each other. This provides some assurance they'll survive the unpredictable dot-com game over the long haul; but it's no guarantee—the management, business idea, and plan still have to stand on their own.

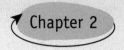

Chapter 2

PRACTICAL HELP
Your Internet Job Tool Kit

Besides being able to convincingly toss off the jargon, there are also some fundamental, easy-to-master skills that will give you the edge in your search. You won't necessarily be knocked out of the game if you *don't* know them, but having these skills under your belt makes it that much easier for a boss to ask, "When can you start?" And once you're through the door, you'll be able to do your job that much better.

Our Top Ten Internet Fundamentals

1. *Get comfortable with your computer's hardware, software, and peripherals.* If you arrive to work your first day and expect someone to show you how to open your e-mail, you may as well go home. Most smaller Internet companies don't have a tech support person to hold your hand on the big stuff, let alone the basics. Get really familiar with the programs loaded on your home computer, even if they're not the same as the ones you'll be using at work. Learn to work with multiple windows open—such as using *Word* at the same time you're logged on to the Web. Try updating your browser software or download some plug-ins off the Internet. You don't have to be a full-out geek, but you can't afford to be a babe in the woods either.

2. *Know how to work a PC.* We know that Macintosh has its rabid supporters, especially among graphic designers and desktop publishing types (not to mention Cindy), but the standard in today's Internet business environment is definitely the IBM-compatible PC. So even if you're wedded to your Mac, borrow a friend's PC for an afternoon. This same thinking applies if you've been relying on Web TV or an Internet appliance for your Internet experience—it's simply not good enough if you're serious about joining the Web world professionally.

3. *Master Microsoft Word.* No matter what your feelings are about Bill Gates as a person, the truth is, this particular software program is pretty much the industry standard. It's simple to learn and will make your transition to the digital world much easier if you—or your potential employers—don't have to keep converting files from some less popular application.

4. *Name files in a way that makes sense.* You'd be surprised at how many times a résumé is e-mailed to an Internet firm as an attachment simply titled "resume.doc." Chances are that same

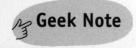 **Geek Note**   When saving an important document to share with someone else, you should almost always save it as a "*.txt"—or text file. Yes, you will lose some pretty formatting, but it will be more universally usable by others and takes up much less disk space. While you're at it, learn the rest of Microsoft *Office.* For sales positions, *PowerPoint* is essential, and most any kind of operations position requires *Excel,* too. Don't stop at learning how to use a spreadsheet to present numbers: Know how to put the formulas in boxes and really work it.

company receives dozens of résumés each month, all with the same file name. It's impossible to distinguish one from the next. Choose less generic names for files; for example, your résumé file should contain *your* name as part of the file name (Jane-Smithresume.doc).

5. *Practice attaching files to e-mail.* Most e-mail programs are fairly self-explanatory on attaching files; usually, there's a button that reads simply "attach file." It leads you through an easy process of finding the file (on the desktop, for example), and clipping it to your e-mail message. Again, remember your formatting may be lost, so send attachments as *.txt (plain text) files. **Important:** scan your computer daily for viruses! There's nothing worse than unwittingly sending an "infected" file attachment to someone. If it's a potential employer, you'll make one heck of a lousy first impression.

6. *Learn to cut and paste documents.* You'll often want to share some tidbit or article with your boss (or someone you want to *become* your boss). The Internet-savvy way is to just cut and paste it into an e-mail message. It's easy to do, so spend a little time playing around with it.

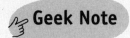 **Geek Note** When you're naming a file think logically. If you're sending a proposal from your company ("Y") to another firm ("X"), think about how *they'll* see it. If you've named it "Proposal X," they may think it's an internal document. Better to name it "Y's Proposal for X." Another tip: Use the most current date when naming files. This is handy if material is being updated by others in your organization. Example: "Y's Proposal for X 9/29/00."

7. *Get a private, non-location-specific e-mail address.* You may already have two e-mail addresses, one for work and one for home. Why get another one? That way you can get and send mail from *anywhere!* When you change jobs or ISPs, you'll never be tied to an ancient e-mail account; and when you're job hunting (which you are), you'll be able to bypass your employer's account to get and send confidential e-mail. There are dozens of places for free e-mail, like Hotmail and Yahoo! Mail. Be professional and use your real name (or something close to it) in this address—save the cute names for another account.

8. *Go shopping.* Even if it's not the main revenue stream of a particular company, e-commerce is key to almost every aspect of Internet business, so find out what all the fuss is about. Buy something online. As you shop, pay attention to every part of the transaction. How easy is it to find items? Are they in stock? Where arc shipping charges hidden? What's the return policy? How does the shopping cart work? Did the site remember you when you visited a second time? How long did it take the merchandise to arrive? What was in the box with it (Amazon, for example, often includes a gift of a free bookmark or fridge magnet)? How were the charges handled? How many times did you get e-mail from the company about your order? Could you track the whereabouts of your package online? Understanding the elements of the e-commerce process is a good thing to know, no matter where in the Internet business you land.

9. *Learn to be a critical web user.* While you're clicking around, *think* about the sites you're looking at and the tools you're using. Which search engine do you use and why? Does the site navigation make sense? How long did the graphics take to load? How hard is it to find what you're looking for? Do

you have to register? Do they give you a good enough reason to do it? Someone somewhere made decisions about all of these issues—do you, as the end user, think they were the right ones? What would you do differently? Questions like these will arise during the interview process, so start developing your own sense of what makes for a great Internet experience.

10. *Learn the vocabulary.* Don't worry—it's a lot easier than your high-school Spanish class ("¿Dondé esta el *browser*?"), and the glossary that follows proves it!

Geek-Free Internet Glossary

If the only Internet phrase you know is "You've got mail!" the idea of actually working in the industry may seem a bit daunting. The common perception is that specialized terms are a lot of techno-babble spoken by people who perform party tricks involving cold fusion physics.

Okay, the Internet business *does* have its own language, much of which is already passing into everyday use: *URLs, dot-coms, links, domains, e-commerce.* This glossary provides a crash course in what you're most apt to hear or read as you immerse yourself in your Internet job hunt . . . and on your first days on the job. We've included most everything we thought you'd find useful, but considering how fast things change, it will be far from comprehensive: It seems as if there's a new term being coined every day! Use our list as your starting point, but read the trade press, newsletters, and Web sites to stay current on the latest additions to the lexicon (see "Resources").

Agnostic: Borrowed from religion. When an Internet person uses it, it usually means they're indifferent to which platform, browser, or operating system is being used. *Example: Our approach to Web design is browser-agnostic.*

Anchor tenant: Big Web sites charge sponsors, advertisers, or partners a large fee to have (usually) category-exclusive placement within certain sections of their site. *Example: The new women's sportswear site negotiated for anchor tenancy on the sports section of AOL.*

Applet: A derivative of the term *application* (which you might hear as *app*—as in "the new killer app"). An applet is a mini-application program that runs something small, like a flashing graphic, versus a larger application, like a spreadsheet program. *Example: That stupid applet keeps crashing my system!*

ASCII (pronounced "as-KEY"): Programming code so basic that every computer—Mac or PC—can read it. *Example: To send a* Word *document in ASCII text, save it as a* *.txt *file.*

ASP (application service provider): One of the big trends in the Internet is outsourcing complicated technical parts of a Web operation. These third-party providers are called ASPs and they offer a huge number of different kinds of software-based services. *Example: Instead of wrestling with e-mail list management, let's outsource it to an ASP.*

Bandwidth: The amount of information, such as text and images, that can be sent through a connection. The more bandwidth you have, the faster those images move. More bandwidth is good, allowing data to move faster and thus appear on your computer faster. Also commonly used to describe a digital worker's ability to take on more projects. *Example: Sorry, I just don't have enough bandwidth to handle that right now.*

Banner: An ad on a Web page. Typically, it's linked to the page of the advertiser, so once you click on it, that's where you're sent. There are standard sizes and formats for these (see chapter 3). *Example: The banner on the top of the page is slowing down the load!*

Beta: A test phase for a site or product; typically, the beta version is still pretty buggy. *Example: When the CEO demonstrates the product for the press, it better be out of beta.*

Bookmark: A way to mark a favorite Web site in your browser so that when you want to return to it, you can simply choose it from a list instead of having to remember its exact URL. Sometimes referred to as "favorite." *Example: How do we get our users to bookmark us so they'll come back often?*

Broadband: Related to bandwidth, it refers to the big fat pipes that allow Web sites to incorporate much cooler and faster applications. *Example: What multimedia have we got in development for our users when they get broadband?*

Browser: The software used to view Web pages. The two biggies are *Netscape* and Microsoft's *Internet Explorer*. *Example: The page looks fine in* Netscape, *but the tables are off in* Explorer.

Business model: An important question to ask about any Internet company. How does it plan to make money? What are its long-term goals? The answers to these and more bottom-line questions fall under its business model. *Example: Their business model included several different revenue streams.*

Cache: Storage area in the hard drive of your computer where recently viewed items are automatically stored. Makes the browsing experience quicker, because the program doesn't have to reload pages from scratch. *Example: If the page doesn't look right, try clearing your cache.*

Chat: A real-time, live, text-based discussion between individuals online. This differs from message boards and bulletin boards, which are merely places to post messages for all to read and respond to. *Example: My pregnancy support group has a chat every Wednesday night at seven.*

Click and mortar: When a brick-and-mortar (not online) company adds an Internet component, they become "click and mortar." Get it? *Example: At a click and mortar, when you order the wrong thing online, you can return it to the store.*

Clicks: The number of times an ad banner is actually clicked on. One derivative of this term is "click-through" (also known as "click rate"), which is the percentage of people viewing a banner who actually clicked it (much more on this in chapter 3). *Example: That silly animated banner got more clicks than all the others.*

Convergence: The trend for computers, televisions, and telecommunications devices to provide overlapping services. You can read your e-mail off your pager or maybe go online during a

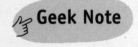 **Geek Note**

If your only experience on the Internet is within AOL, now's the time to go further. You can get to the Web itself through AOL. *Internet Explorer* is usually bundled with most Microsoft software (like Microsoft Office). *Netscape* is commonly included on the desktop of new computers or with service from your ISP. Installation is literally as easy as clicking on the icon, so don't be intimidated. And once you've got one or both of the browsers, keep them current by upgrading to the latest versions to get all the bells and whistles.

TV show to purchase an outfit that one of the characters is wearing. *Example: Oxygen is all about convergence of cable TV and the Web.*

Cookie: An invisible marker that literally tracks your activity on the Web. When you visit a site, you are given an electronic "cookie" that tells Web marketers when you've visited and lets them gather data on your activity. This has been a great source of controversy for DoubleClick and privacy advocates. **Note:** You can disable this feature in your browser. *Example: When I visited that site, it cookie'd me so that it recognized me when I came back.*

CPM (cost per thousand): What a Web site charges for guaranteeing that so many thousand viewers will see an ad banner. If a

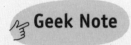

Geek Note Chat rooms require a kind of shorthand, because, after all, you're typing really fast! *Emoticons* are the little faces you make by typing in groups of punctuation marks. The trick to interpreting these is to tilt your head sideways to the left and look for a recognizable facial expression such as :). Then there are these commonly used abbreviations:

BBL: be back later
BRB: be right back
BTW: by the way
FOTFL: falling on the floor laughing
GMTA: great minds think alike
IMHO: in my humble opinion
IRL: in real life
LOL: laugh out loud
OIC: oh, I see
ROFL: rolling on the floor laughing
TEOTWAWKI: the end of the world as we know it

site charges $20,000 for a banner and delivers it to 500,000 pages, their CPM is $40 (do the math: $20,000 divided by 500). *Example: Targeted sites can get away with charging a high CPM because their audience is so focused on the topic.*

Cyber: Prefix denoting things to do with the Web. Most Internet people don't use this much anymore because it sounds *so* 1995. So learn it but don't use it much. *Example: None. We just told you, don't use it!*

Day trading: An individual (not a broker) who uses the Internet to buy and sell stocks himself or herself. This is certainly a good way to spend some time—but probably not a great way to make a living. We mention it here so that there's no confusion. Day trading is not an Internet business (most day traders lose money). *Example: My brother-in-law quit his job to start day trading and now he won't leave the spare bedroom, where he watches four monitors simultaneously.*

Digital divide: Phrase used by politicians to denote the schism in society between the people with access to personal computers and the Internet and those who don't. *Example: Bill Gates is giving computers to libraries to help narrow the digital divide.*

Domain: That little tag that goes at the end of a URL: .com for commercial sites, .edu for educational, .org for organizations, .net for networks, .gov for U.S. government sites, and .mil for the U.S. military. You might also run across two-letter domains representing countries, such as .uk for the United Kingdom. New ones are coming. *Example: If you want to build a new site, log on to find out if the domain name is still available.*

Drill down: Used in the site creation context, it means clicking through various layers of Web content to find what you're looking for. Also used as a general business phrase, meaning "let's get down to brass tacks." *Example: If users have to drill down too far to find their topic, we'll lose them.*

DSL (digital subscriber line): High-speed Internet access over your plain old telephone lines. *Example: I didn't need an extra phone line for Internet access after they hooked up my DSL line.*

e: Frequently stuck on the front of words to make them seem wired and cool. *Examples: e-business, e-banking, e-tailing.*

Early adopters: The technophiles who try everything first. They were the first ones to get Palm Pilots or wireless Web access over their cell phones; they discover cool new technology and tell everyone else about it. *Example: Let's see how the early adopters use our site before we launch it to the public.*

Eudora: One of the more popular e-mail programs. *Example: I got your file, it's in my Eudora attachment folder.*

FAQ (frequently asked questions): Many Web sites feature this section to answer the issues that come up most often. You can save yourself a lot of time by checking this part of a site out first. *Example: If we make our FAQ thorough, we won't need as many customer service reps.*

Firewall: Protects the inner workings of a computer system or network from unauthorized access by outsiders. *Example: Hackers won't be able to get at our users' registration info as long as our firewall stays secure.*

First mover advantage: The benefits of being first to market with a particular product or niche. *Example: The VC's estimate on our first mover advantage should net us an extra $3 million in funding.*

Flame: In a chat, board, or newsgroup, any message to another that's derogatory or attacking, especially if it attacks the recipient personally versus the issue at hand. *Example: Just because he disagreed with my opinion, there was no cause for such a nasty flame.*

Friends and family (F&F): Exalted status to have, if you know people who have started an Internet company that's about to go public. If you're put on their F&F list, you'll be given the opportunity to buy shares in the company at the initial offering price. *Example: Old acquaintances came out of the woodwork before we went IPO, begging to be put on my friends and family list!*

FTP (file transfer protocol): Simply a way of moving, downloading, or sending files from one Internet site to another, or to someone's hard drive. *Example: I was working from home and FTP'd those files to the client yesterday.*

GIF (graphic interchange format): Say *jiff*. This is the format used for most photos, illustrations, and images you see on the Web. (See also *JPEG*.) *Example: That animated GIF made the banner lively.*

GUI (graphical user interface): Pronounced *gooey*. Also just called the "user interface" (UI). Describes what the designers and producers do to help the user know what to do on a Web site. *Example: The GUI on that database search just confused the visitors.*

Hit: A method—admittedly a poor one—of measuring traffic to a Web site. Every element you, as a user, see on a Web page generates a "hit" in the server's log. Thus a page with two graphic elements on it measures three hits: one for the page itself and one for each graphic. Best used by Webmasters to monitor their server's workload. Try not to use this word, because Internet professionals rarely measure anything by hits. *Example: Too many hits at one time might bring the server down.*

Host: The actual computer that is hooked into the Internet, which your provider is using to give you access to the Web. *Example: Our Web site is hosted at a server farm in New Jersey.*

HTML (hypertext markup language): This is the coded format used to create Web documents. HTML commands control how the words and images display on the end user's screen. Newer yet are extensible or dynamic markup language (XML or DHTML). *Example: If you don't know HTML, you'll never get a job as a Web producer.*

Hypertext/hyperlink: You'll see these on a Web page, either highlighted or underlined. By clicking on them, you're sent to another site that is linked to the original one. *Example: If you're going to put that hyperlink up to another site, check and make sure it works.*

i: Used to denote "interactivity," thus coolness (see also *e.*) *Examples: i-chat, ivillage.*

ICANN (Internet Corporation for Assigned Names and Numbers): The folks responsible for domain names. *Example: ICANN has to decide whether to create more and different suffixes.*

Icon: A graphical element that usually represents a major function or feature on a Web site. *Example: The icon for e-mail is usually a mailbox or a letter.*

Information superhighway: Phrase coined in the early 1990s to denote the cool new world of the Web. No one ever uses this. *Example: Really, no one ever, ever uses this.*

Instant messaging: Software that lets individuals chat privately in real time with others on their designated list. The big ones are ICQ and Instant Messenger. *Example: When I see my boss come on to instant messaging, I prepare for a barrage of small talk.*

Interstitials: Those annoying pop-up ads that greet you on some Web sites. *Example: Advertisers love interstitials because they're so obtrusive.*

Intranet: A Web site that is meant for limited access, typically within a single company. *Example: Joe can access his employee benefit information over the company Intranet.*

IP (internet protocol) address: Every system hooked into the Internet has a unique one of these made up of numbers and decimal points. Usually handled automatically by your ISP or network administrator when you log on. *Example: You may need to know your IP address to access your work e-mail from home.*

ISDN (integrated services digital network): A superfast digital phone line with two channels that lets you get online at speeds up to 128 kbps. *Example: The ISDN order took three weeks for the phone company to process.*

ISP (internet service provider): These are the folks who connect you to the Internet via a dial-up phone number—and usually charge a monthly fee for the service. Juno and Earthlink are ISPs. *Example: My ISP has local numbers across the country so I can access it wherever I travel.*

Java: A versatile programming language that allows things to work on any computer platform or any browser. *Example: That Java applet really rocks!*

JPEG: Say *jay-peg*. A graphics format that makes graphic files smaller, so they download faster. (See also *GIF*.) *Example: My wife just uploaded a JPEG of my baby, wanna see?*

LAN (local area network): Typically, a single office is wired together into a LAN for sharing files, printers, etc. *Example: The LAN is coming down for service, so save your files now.*

Link: See *Hyperlink*.

Linux (Pronounced *LYNN-ucks*): A rival operating system to Microsoft's ubiquitous Windows operating system. Cutting-edge Web developers love this freeware and it's making major inroads into Microsoft's turf. *Example: RedHat Software is the biggest proponent of Linux.*

Listserv: One of the biggest commercial automatic mailing list servers. Messages are transmitted via e-mail to only the names on one of Listserv's mailing lists. (See also *Mailing list*.) *Example: Listserv is just one mailing list program; Majordomo is another one.*

Load: Whenever you access a Web site, its graphics and text are loaded into the browser for you to view them. *Example: Image-heavy pages are slow to load.*

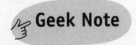 **Geek Note** Just like a trendy New York club or Kate Spade handbags, status has entered the online world. How you access the Internet sends a message about your hip quotient. AOL is the lowest of the low entry levels, so please take our advice and get another e-mail address that is not associated with your work or your ISP.

Login: The act of typing your user name and/or password to access an ISP or particular Web site. *Example: Login and see if you got the same error message I did.*

Lurker/lurking: When visitors come to a site that requires registration, they decide not to register and participate but to read the posts and stay in the background—just like the real-world equivalent. Also when subscribers to a mailing list or newsgroup read messages but do not post. *Example: If only we could get all those message board lurkers to become members, we'd double our registration!*

m: Sometimes added to the front of words to indicate "mobile." (See also *e* and *i*.) *Example: m-browsing is Web browsing on a mobile phone.*

Mailing list: A discussion group to which members subscribe. The lists are generally focused on a particular topic, and members receive messages via e-mail. (See also *Listserv.*) *Example: The mailing list on raising cactus plants is growing every week.*

Message board: Also known as a "discussion" or "bulletin" board. Messages are posted on a particular subject for all parties to read and respond to if they wish. This differs from "chat," which is real-time, live discussion. *Example: The message boards have a great thread going about whether that famous ballplayer should have been suspended or not.*

Metrics: Generally means measurement of almost anything in the Internet space. One of the big controversies as the industry has evolved is the lack of consistent measurement and tracking of any specific relevant numbers. *Example: The weekly magazine* Industry Standard *has an excellent "metrics" section, which gives a lot of insight into the new media economy.*

Modem: The piece of hardware (internal or external) that allows your computer to link to the Internet via cable or phone line. Measured in kilobits per second (kbps, for short). If you're using a modem, 56k or faster (a higher number) is standard, but lots of people use older computers that go much slower. *Example: My modem is so slow that I watch TV while I'm on the Web.*

Monetizing: Turning an idea into money. *Example: It's great that our site has a million registered members; now how do we monetize them?*

MP3: An audio technology for the Web. *Example: I downloaded that new band's song onto my portable MP3 player.*

Multitasking: Person or a computer doing more than one thing at a time; a basic skill all Internet workers must have. *Example: I was multitasking by being on that conference call as I rewrote the presentation.*

Napster: Controversial music-swapping program that lets you download/trade your favorite tunes from another user's hard drive.

Netiquette: The Internet version of etiquette. These are the general rules a user abides by, especially when participating in a newsgroup or mailing list discussion. For example, it's good netiquette to look at the FAQ section before bothering other members with questions that may have already been answered. And be sure to AVOID TYPING IN ALL CAPS. It looks like you're shouting. *Example: When she asked that question, she violated the rules of netiquette.*

Newsgroup: Similar to a bulletin board. A discussion forum in which members post and reply to messages on a particular topic, such as whale watching or tech stocks. *Example: My health newsgroup pointed me to a great article on nutritional remedies.*

NT: Short for Microsoft's Windows NT Operating System, one of the standards for business and high-tech applications including Web servers. *Example: Make sure the Web developer knows we're running Apache on an NT box.*

Offline: Anything in the world that is not online. And in general use, it means "Let's not interrupt what we're doing here to talk about that topic. Let's do it when everyone else isn't in the room . . . and it's not on the record." *Example: Can we talk about your option package offline?*

Operating system: Just what it sounds like, the system that runs a computer. Most PCs use some variation on Microsoft's Windows operating system. Rivals are Apple and Linux. *Example: Windows 2000 is a recent version of Microsoft's PC operating system.*

Page views: A more precise measure than the term *hits*. This denotes the number of times a user accesses a Web page, which in turn may (or may not) indicate how often a particular ad was potentially seen ("gross impressions"). *Example: What can we do to up our page views in Media Metrix this month?*

PDA (personal digital assistant): The handheld computers everyone's walking around with—mostly Palm Pilots, but lots of new ones are coming out, many of which act as your phone and your Web access, too. *Example: My PDA pinged to remind me of our appointment.*

Personalization: Customizing the Web experience to each individual visitor based on his or her interests and preferences.

Example: When you make a repeat visit to Amazon, you're greeted with personalized suggestions based on what you have looked at before.

Platform: The type of computer or operating system on which a software application runs, such as PC, Mac, or Unix. *Example: Tell the designer it has to look good on all platforms!*

Plug-in: Small programs that you need to add on ("plug in," get it?) to your browser to be able to use their functionality. *Example: The* Comet Cursor *is a plug-in that lets you change your cursor to all kinds of cool icons.*

Portal: A Web site trying to do it all, like providing services (news, weather, and other content) and a search engine for other links to other sites. *Example: Yahoo is the biggest portal out there.*

Preferences: Allows you to choose certain parameters within your browser, such as how the text will appear in your e-mail messages, your e-mail name, etc. *Example: You can change the start page of your browser by editing your preferences menu.*

Pure play: A company that did not exist before the Internet. A pure play business doesn't rely on non-Internet revenue streams to support it. *Example: Amazon is a pure play; bn.com is not.*

Real Audio/Real Video: Technologies that let you listen to music or view movies over the Internet, both products of Real Networks. Bundled with the most recent versions of browsers, otherwise you need to get a plug-in. *Example: Let's add a* Real Audio *stream of music clips to make this piece more interesting.*

Scalability: How capable is this system of handling a lot more users and load than it gets now? *Example: Before we run that sweepstakes, let's make sure the system is scalable.*

Search engine: Literally a program that searches a digital database of any kind; commonly used to refer to Web sites that specialize in searching the Internet for specific information or Web sites on a specified topic. *Example: Some search engines use artificial intelligence to sort results; some just do a literal search.*

Server: The host computer on a network. May also refer to the software that allows for "serving" of information. *Example: If the server crashes, our site will be down. What's the backup?*

Shareware: Software available for downloading that lets you test-drive it before you buy it. If you decide to keep using it, you may have to pay a fee for which you'll get technical support and updated versions. Conversely, "freeware" is software you can download for—you guessed it—free. *Example: Try the shareware and make sure the program does what you want it to.*

Shockwave: A technology that allows Web sites to show really sophisticated graphics, often animated. If you have an old browser, you may need a plug-in, but it's not necessary if you have the most recent version of your browser software (the plug-in is probably bundled in). This is one of many fancy software applications that makes Web sites more fun to play with. *Example: That Shockwave game kept me playing for hours.*

Sidebar: On a Web site, something you put to the side to cover other issues flanking the main topic. In everyday talk, it means "Let's take this conversation off to the side." *Example: Let's put all the relevant links on the topic over there in the sidebar.*

Signature file: A file that's automatically attached to your outgoing e-mail or postings to a newsgroup. *Example: Your business sig-*

nature file should always include your full e-mail address, company, title, and phone number.

Snail mail: To the *digerati*, any method of delivery that is physical, like the U.S. Postal Service or UPS. *Example: Can you believe they snail-mailed the agenda to me?*

Soft launch: When a Web site is ready to go but not ready to announce to the public, it will go live but those first days (or months) will be called a soft launch. *Example: Let's gauge user reaction to the new interface during the soft launch before we send out the press release.*

Spam: "Junk" e-mail. Can also mean adding unwanted postings to a newsgroup with no regard as to whether the material is relevant. *Example: Once you register at several sites, it won't be long till your inbox is clogged with spam.*

Splash page: A first screen that visitors may see when they come to a site, it's often something dramatic like an animated logo that draws the users into the content. *Example: Their splash page makes quite an impression for that site development firm.*

Sticky: Used to describe how good a site is at keeping you with them once you arrive, by offering other resources and tools that are relevant. *Example: The real estate site added a mortgage calculator and live chat with a local broker to make their site more sticky.*

Streaming media: A technique to send video and audio over the Internet. A constant stream of images or sounds provided on demand. *Example: You can find hundreds of radio stations online, all offering their programs in streaming format.*

T-1/T-3: An ultra-high-speed network connection to the Internet. T-3 is even faster than T-1. *Example: Is my laptop hooked up to the office T-1?*

Take-away: The bottom line, the most important thing. *Example: The take-away on that discussion was that we need to call the agency for new branding ideas right away.*

Unique users: The number of different people who visit a site in a specific time period, a measure of reach on the Internet. They may be identified via a registration process or by cookies. *Example: How is our unique user count compared to the competition?*

UNIX: A computer operating system, frequently used by Web-serving computers. *Example: The techies often prefer UNIX to Windows NT.*

URL (uniform resource locator): All you really need to remember is that a URL is the exact address you type to reach a particular Web site. *Example: If it doesn't have an easy-to-spell URL, the site's doomed.*

Verticals: Shorthand for vertical markets in the Internet world. Business development types throw this term around all the time. *Example: The senior management team has experience in the used-car-parts vertical.*

Viral marketing: Your users and members get other users and members for your site or product with very little effort on your part. *Example: Hotmail is the ultimate viral marketing tool. When you send someone a message, at the bottom of the e-mail, it encourages the recipient to sign up for his or her own Hotmail account.*

Virus: A bad, bad thing. A program that infects a file or a whole computer and can damage everything in its wake. Very easy to send unwittingly through e-mail or an attachment. *Example: Use virus-protection software every day to make sure you don't unwittingly make any enemies.*

Visits: A sequence of information requests made by a user at a Web site. That entire sequence counts as a "visit." If there's no activity for a specified time-out period (usually thirty minutes) and that same user then starts working with the site again, that's considered a new visit. *Example: If the community leader posts new items every day, she'll encourage repeat visits.*

Virtual: Refers to objects, activities, and the like that take place in cyberspace, such as "virtual" malls. *Example: Some companies don't have physical offices, their employees all work virtually.*

WAP (wireless applications protocol): Allows wireless and handheld gadgets to handle complicated Web browsing and transactions. *Example: My new cell phone is WAP-enabled.*

WWWAC (World Wide Web Artists' Consortium): One of the more active online organizations that acts as a virtual community for many offsite and freelance creative types. *Example: You can frequently find interesting job leads on the WWWAC list.*

Zip: Shorthand for compressing a file to make it easier to transmit or store. The sender and recipient both need compatible compression and decompression software to zip and unzip files. *Example: Cindy's Zip drive was our backup for the whole book.*

Did we miss anything? We covered the basics of what you need to know—plus plenty of stuff we hear thrown around the office every day—but we urge you to keep current by reading everything you can about the industry. If you find something else you'd like us to define, e-mail authors@notjustgeeks.com.

Now let's move on and get into the nitty-gritty of what your present job looks like on the virtual side.

YOUR JOB, ONLY BETTER

What's your brick-and-mortar job right now? How can you translate that into an Internet job? That's what this section is all about!

Each of the following nine chapters discusses a general "department" or hiring area most Internet companies use to organize themselves. This industry is a work-in-progress, and these areas are likely to evolve; but as of this writing, we've covered the biggest ones that we know of. Of course, our Web site (http://www.notjustgeeks.com) allows us to provide the very latest information on this fast-changing industry.

What you'll find in each chapter is a wealth of information gleaned from talking to many, many people on the inside of this Internet mecca. What you *won't* find are techie jobs like programming, Web producing, or systems analyst positions. Although they're a vital part of the Internet world, the title of this book pretty much says it all. These are jobs *for the rest of us.*

We're also not addressing high-powered senior-management types angling to become the next president of eBay or Amazon. This info is for average working folks like you who just want to get in the game; but no matter where you're at now or what you aspire to, there's plenty of information here that will serve you well.

Now read on for the lowdown about:

- **Sales:** Even if you've been in sales before, what's the same, what's different in the Internet game?
Internet experience required: preferred, but not required.

- **Business development:** Work with other companies to make yours a big success.
Internet experience required: preferred, not required.

- **Operations:** Even Internet companies need toilet paper.
Internet experience required: none.

- **Creative:** Writers, editors, art directors, and designers actually get to build the Web site.
Internet experience required: some familiarity needed.

- **Advertising and marketing:** Can you make your dot-com break out from the pack? You'll get lots of money to try.
Internet experience required: none.

- **e-Commerce:** Know how to merchandise an end-of-aisle display? Or deal with irate customers? Find out what's the same and what's different in the Internet space.
Internet experience required: none.

- **Law, public relations, and community:** There are some key differences in how these particular jobs work on the Web.
Internet experience required: varies.

- **Miscellaneous:** It's a big Internet world—bring what you already know.
Internet experience required: none.

- **Internet jobs at traditional companies:** Try your hand in any of these hiring areas . . . at a company that makes money the old-fashioned way.
Internet experience required: varies.

Some General Observations

Think broadly about the possibilities. A large component of the Internet world is "versatility," so we suggest you read up on more than just one hiring area. Who knows? You may surprise yourself with an interest in something altogether different. Plus, within each broad hiring area, there's a lot of variety. For example, a sales position at a software company is likely to be different from a sales position in a publishing company. When you're breaking into this game, you need to understand these differences.

Think big picture. No matter what your specific job title is within an Internet company, you'll be expected to have a broad understanding of what the industry is all about, how a particular firm fits into it, and how each department affects the others. This is an ever-changing business: Never assume that because you understand your particular job function you don't have to continue to learn about and to evolve with everything that's happening both inside and outside your company.

Learn to juggle. The atmosphere is high intensity, and you'll probably be required to handle many different projects simultaneously.

There is a low risk way to try all of this. If Internet work sounds exciting, but you're not quite ready to jump into a pure play, consider transferring into the Internet department of your present firm or of another traditional company. This is often the easiest first move for a newcomer. It's a great way to gain knowledge and experience without sacrificing job security.

☞ THRIVING IN THE INTERNET WORLD

While writing this book, we ran across this in *Business Week E-Biz* (February 2000) and thought it pretty much summed up what it takes to survive in the Internet business world no matter which career path you choose. So here are the characteristics, as determined by a survey of the Net's best executives, that will help you climb the virtual ladder a lot faster:

* *Seize the moment*. Learn to jump on new business concepts and innovations ASAP.

* *Radiate vision*. Keep the long-term strategy in mind—and talk it up whenever possible to the team.

* *Work the new 80/20 rule*. If you're given only 80 percent of the data, learn to draw on your experience and insight to fill in the blanks.

* *Stay focused*. Keep your eye on the aspects of the business model that generate revenue, and don't get sucked into make-work tasks with little payoff.

* *Be an organizational improviser*. Push ideas, not hierarchy, and be fluid enough to respond to customer needs or competitive shifts in a heartbeat.

* *Become learning obsessed*. Take it upon yourself to learn about a situation firsthand—don't just take a course or delegate. Keep reexamining your assumptions and challenging what you know.

Now settle in for our virtual tour of great Internet careers!

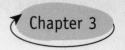

Chapter 3

SALES
Follow the Money

This might be the right place for you if your job right now is:

- Media advertising salesperson of any kind
- Manufacturer's representative
- Inside or outside salesperson
- Sales management
- Sales support staff
- Sales specialist
- Sales presentation staff
- Account executive

Overview

To simplify the discussion, we've organized Internet sales jobs into two basic categories. Most positions fall into one or the other of the following: ad sales or service/products sales.

AD SALES

One of the principal business models for Internet companies is advertising sales, particularly for companies that produce content and for search engines and portals. It's only recently that this revenue stream has really taken off, because Internet companies and traditional advertisers have begun to spend money to attract visitors to their Web sites and build their brands.

The Internet has advertisers excited because of its potential to highly target customers and gather valuable marketing data not easily delivered through other media. Granted, the technology for doing it—and tracking effectiveness—is still a work in progress, but it's come a long way from the days when each Web site randomly chose what size and formats of banners to run. Now there are clear standards, and most sites conform to those rules.

The ad-supported revenue model is more established now—some companies are actually profitable! Because the success or failure of the ad sales department is mission critical to the financial success of the enterprise, most companies focus a lot of attention on it and are always looking for capable sales staff. In addition, there's burgeoning territory for Internet sales within advertising rep firms and advertising network sales. All in all, it's a very fertile area for hiring.

SERVICES, SOFTWARE, AND HARDWARE SALES

Besides media, there's another area of sales within the Internet game. Many new companies are business-to-business (B2B). They offer the hosting service, the ad-serving software, or the latest customer-service package to make running an Internet business more productive. Some sell these solutions to traditional companies as well as to Web clients. For instance, a Web development shop may need account executives to sell its design and development services to brick-and-mortar companies that haven't got-

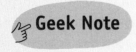 **Geek Note**   For some general information about advertising on the Internet, the Internet Advertising Bureau is a good place to start (http://www.iab.net).

ten on the Web yet. An ASP needs to sell its shopping cart solution to companies adding e-commerce as a sales channel.

Service and software companies need to quickly prove themselves with real revenue—and the sales department is at the heart of it. Unlike media sales, it may require more technical expertise on the salesperson's part to effectively sell the service. After all, if *you* don't understand what it does, you won't stand a chance of selling it to anyone else.

What the Work Is Like

Whether it's an ad banner or a software package, a salesperson at an Internet company is expected to do two things:

Know the company, Web site, and products very well.

Try to meet the clients' business needs by matching them to the product or service.

So far, so good. But then the resemblance to a traditional sales job ends. For example, you may or may not have an established client list. If you're lucky enough to have one, all may not be as it appears. An ad salesperson, for example, will have to discover whether the client buys direct or uses an agency. Is that agency the same one that does the client's other advertising or is it an Internet-only agency? Of course, the *really* fun part is if your client has never bought Web advertising before; then you must educate him or her about the Internet and its benefits before you even get to present your ideas. From content to hardware, the Internet is constantly evolving. Salespeople must stay on top of what's happening at their company. If you're selling ad space, you may discover that the sponsorship package you so elaborately outlined in a multimedia presentation last week has suddenly become obsolete because the programming staff eliminated the section of the site that you were pitching. And anyone who's ever upgraded his or her computer software knows how fast equipment and technology changes: Software or hardware salespeople must stay current.

As a salesperson, you'll most likely have little or no support staff and will do all your own presentations. If you don't know it already, learn Microsoft *PowerPoint*. And start doing those bicep curls: You'll be schlepping your laptop and projector all over the place for your dog-and-pony show.

Internet sales requires a level of creativity, innovation, and problem solving not always drawn on in traditional sales. If you do well, you'll not only be making great money but be on the fast track. A hot Internet salesperson is always in demand. Plus, no one gets more immediate feedback on a company or its product than the feet on the street; as a salesperson, you'll be an important player in the company's game plan. Sounds fun, doesn't it?

David vs. Goliath Issues

The biggest difference between Davids and Goliaths is that those with no Internet experience probably can't get hired at a Goliath firm. The largest Internet companies can limit applicant pools to those who already have some Internet or software sales history. There are exceptions, of course; but if you get your first Internet gig with a Goliath, you can bet it will be much more narrowly defined.

In Goliath companies, people aren't wearing as many hats as they do at a start-up, "and that hat will become much smaller and more specialized," according to one of our sources. There's not as much of a call for that scrappy, I-want-to-do-it-all attitude. On the other hand, David companies *will* let you do it all—in fact, they *need* you to do it all because you'll probably be the entire sales department.

Working at one of these start-ups is a priceless learning experience: You'll be helping set strategy and choose market segments and influencing the direction of your company. However, if you're the first hire, count on your first few months to be mostly setup and preparation for the actual sales effort. You may have to make a pitch without a kit, rate cards, or other backup materials until you help create them. If you're not comfortable with that type of seat-of-the-pants sales, shy away from a David firm.

Key Characteristics of Successful People in This Specialty

INNOVATIVE AND CREATIVE

If you're used to traditional media sales, such as newspapers or magazines, you already know the drill with the media buyer—and they know the traditional media turf. Selling an Internet site will require going the extra mile, teaching buyers what they need to know about your Web site, who it attracts, what the concept is, and why it's a good fit for their client.

For software and services sales, you may frequently call on others as new to this world as you are! So the sales process will require improvising as you adjust to the skill and knowledge level of the person in front of you.

All of this is particularly tough when you're representing a site or product so new that you have nothing to back it up with. You may be selling a service no one ever thought of before. Or you'll go in as the second or third offering in a very specific category and need to fight for mind share. It won't be easy and will rarely mean you're a simple order taker. This fact alone separates the men from the boys (and to be democratic, the women from the "grrrls").

SOLUTION ORIENTED

One of the much-hyped benefits of Internet advertising is its increasing ability to target customers. A good salesperson must understand the many ways he or she can use the new technology to address the client's needs.

For example, if your client complains there's not enough traffic to his or her ad, what do you do to fix it? One of our experts warns, "Don't get stuck on 'Here's our banner, here's our rate card.' We're rapidly entering a place where it's not just the quantity of eyeballs or users, it's the quality."

In software sales, you may need to bring a techie with you to show it off (he or she is probably the only one who understands it anyway). Listen to your customers, then show them how your product addresses their needs.

OPEN TO TECHNOLOGY

The Internet is all about change. Even if you don't understand the geek stuff, you must be willing to learn about new developments. If you're tech shy, stick with ad sales, where you can get away with less expertise. For hardware, software, and other Internet services, however, if you can't become conversant in your product, you won't be successful.

What to Expect Once You Start the Job

DON'T EXPECT A LIST OF ACCOUNTS . . . OR MUCH ELSE

Most traditional salespeople are accustomed to receiving a list of existing accounts when they start. This isn't necessarily the case in the Internet world. You'll most likely be expected to drum up new business on your own—and almost all business in Internet space is by definition, "new business"! Therefore, your old Rolodex may be of little help in getting you started.

For ad sales, if you *are* given a list, it's very possible it includes companies that don't do much Internet advertising, so you'll end up doing a fair amount of educating clients, agencies, and media buyers.

In the software and services categories, the world is wide open. So many Internet players are sprouting up—and these are companies that are often potential targets for what you're selling. Don't forget the brick and mortars that might need your product or service, too. Before you accept the job, make sure you understand any limitations on the geography or category of businesses you'll be allowed to pitch.

A MORE CASUAL ATMOSPHERE

Even with the Goliaths, there's generally a more relaxed environment extending from dress codes to the times meetings actually get started. It's a natural offshoot of the constant activity engulfing the Internet business. If you're the truly buttoned-down type, keep this in mind.

NO HIGH-PRICED SCHMOOZING

Salespeople accustomed to fat entertainment budgets for wining and dining clients are in for a shock. This is down-and-dirty sales with a very short sales cycle. If you depend on pricey lunches or front-row concert tickets to help you close a deal, think carefully about jumping to Internet sales.

Don't Get Hung Up On

KNOWING ALL THE LINGO OR TECHNOLOGY

You'll learn much of it on the fly. Plus, every company uses a different back-end technology and has its own definitions. The competitive set changes constantly—you'll get familiar with it once you get started.

DON'T WORRY ABOUT THE DETAILS . . . YET

Our experts generally agree that if a candidate has a successful sales background and some basic knowledge of the Internet, the details are easy to learn on the job: "I think from there, everything else can be learned, but they at least have to understand what the Internet is," says one. Another tells us, "My training for salespeople is two days, and they're selling on the third. I don't care so much about the technical, it's more important that they understand the different business models of the Internet and what each is trying to do." If you need to, head back to chapter 1 for a quick review of Internet business models.

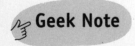 **Geek Note** Get familiar with the world of Internet advertising if you want a job selling it. See which sites are selling their inventory well (Yahoo, Lycos, AOL, and iVillage are some great examples). Who are their advertisers? Are these the same companies that spend money on traditional media or are they different brands and companies?

Typical Compensation

Internet salespeople are in great demand and command excellent pay, particularly in overheated media markets like New York and San Francisco. Base salary is competitive with other sales jobs. Then there's the commission: A good salesperson with a great site or a great product can double his or her salary, even in the first year. Even David companies will have to give you a solid base and the chance to go up from there. And, of course, everyone qualifies for the stock option plan!

Commissions range from 3 to 10 percent of sales. Goliath companies can pay less, because you'll sell more and it's higher priced. The commission rates may be tied to meeting the sales plan (e.g., you'll command higher rates if you exceed it). Yes, the usual mishmash of complicated commissions and bonuses has found its way onto the Internet.

If you're going to work at an early-stage David, do your best to negotiate some period (three to six months at least) with a reward linked to all the setup and systems you'll have to put in place before you can start selling. Then you can assess the market and make sure the product is salable.

A David that's in start-up mode might not be in the position to come up with a realistic commission plan before you start selling: It may well be that you and the founder come up with the plan once you're already out in the market. Just make sure your expectations are in line with management's so that when you agree on your comp plan, there aren't any unpleasant surprises. And get it all in writing!

Interview Questions and Concerns to Be Prepared For

- What sites do you regularly visit? Why do you like them? What's good or bad about them?

- What do you think of our site? What's good, what's bad?

- What do you think of our competitors' sites? What's different, what's good, what's bad?

- Give me your impressions of our sales offering.

- How do you currently generate your leads? (In answering this question, show that you think about the big picture and about which categories of clients suit the product.)

- How do you research clients?

- Discuss the innovative ways you've solved problems for your clients in the past.

- Give an example of how you worked as a member of a team to accomplish a goal.

- Tell me about a client you prospected from the ground up.

- How do you exceed your client's expectations?

Get to Know

You'll find more general information in "Resources," but the following Web sites are targeted specifically to sales.

- http://www.channelseven.com
Great *Narrowcast* newsletter; the Ad/Insight page is just for ad sales.

- http://www.adage.com
Ad sales and marketing types should be looking at this every day. *Interactive Daily* has the news on the Internet marketplace.

- http://cyberatlas.internet.com
Good reference information on the industry, top Web site lists, industry analysis. Has the best demographics, basic industry info, plus specialized coverage (online financial, etc.).

- http://www.digitrends.net
This is the online site of a great magazine.

- http://www.businessmarketing.com
B2B Internet ad and marketing news.

- http://www.iab.net/events/eventsource.html
Good list, by category, of various industry events.

- http://www.ad-guide.com
Good lists of resources, including Web marketing firms and event listings.

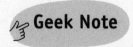 **Geek Note** Here's a neat trick for networking. Rather than paying big registration fees for an industry event, crash the cocktail parties and receptions. They don't check badges then and most people hang around to schmooze.

Deep Background

Here are some key terms and concepts for Internet advertising.

Measurement: page views, impressions, unique visitors. When you are selling Internet advertising, you are selling one of these. Understand what they are and what the differences among them are.

Rates: CPM, cost per action, sponsorships. The price you're charging is either a CPM for total number of impressions, or a cost per action (either a click or a transaction of some sort at the other end). Big Web sites get away without promising any performance and just selling a high-end sponsorship or anchor position for which they charge a premium. However, pay-for-performance deals—in which an advertiser pays per click or per visit—are becoming more common.

Advertising formats. Banner sizes are standardized now. Top banners are 468×60 pixels and buttons or tiles are one of several sizes (120×90, 120×60, or 125×125). There are also interstitials, daughter windows, and rich media and more are being invented all the time.

Branding vs. click rate. The great debate in the Internet business. When the Internet was new (and so were the users), ad banners got click-through rates of 3 to 5 percent (maybe because no one knew what they were doing). The rate is below .05 percent now, and marketers make a case for the power of the ad banner to help with branding, even if the consumers don't click the banner to go to the client's Web site.

Conversion rate. Once you get visitors to your site, what percentage of them do what you want them to do?

Where Can You Go from Here?

Salespeople are well equipped to move into entirely different positions in an Internet company, particularly into business development.

The key piece of advice from those we talked to is not to limit your attention to your job responsibilities alone, or even your department's. Traditional companies may have clear divisions—sales, production, etc.—whose paths rarely cross, but in an Internet organization, things overlap. Your success will depend on being able to view your role in the larger entity and a willingness to step outside the box.

ALSO READ

Chapter 4: Business Development
Chapter 7: Advertising and Marketing
Chapter 8: E-Commerce

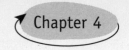

BUSINESS DEVELOPMENT
Calling All Dealmakers

This might be the right place for you if your job right now is:

- Salesperson
- Affiliate relations manager
- Syndication manager
- Account executive

- Attorney
- Contract administrator
- Marketing department
- Membership manager

Overview

With no exact parallel in traditional firms, business development plays a unique role in the Internet industry. The coolest software application or neatest concept for a Web site can't go anywhere without strategic direction; in other words, without an answer to the question, "How do we turn this kernel of an idea into a real business?" Many companies have gotten funded without ever actually building out the product; at some level it's more important to know what you plan to do with it once it's built. This goes to the heart of business development and why it's so mission critical to the success of an Internet venture. You set the whole course for the company, then make it happen.

The Internet has grown organically as sites, groups, and companies link together in interesting and creative ways. The business development group (or "Biz Dev" if you want to be hip) is generally responsible for pursuing the liaisons and relationships with both Web companies and traditional firms. That could mean standard affiliation relationships, tenancy agreements on portals, content licensing agreements, cross-marketing deals, or tire kicking on possible acquisitions. AOL and Sears cross-market each other; McDonald's hooked up with food.com. The possibilities are endless: If, for example, you're working deals for a David and manage to align yourself with a big player like Microsoft, you could literally ensure the success of your company. Pretty heady stuff!

Because this is a brand-new department in a brand-new industry, business development requires innovative thinking beyond that of other Internet jobs. But, as we just mentioned, it can also be the most rewarding role at an Internet company as you help steer your firm to greatness.

What the Work Is Like

The Biz Dev folks need to keep their eye on the Internet landscape at all times for the next deal. Whether the company is big or small, this is an essential function and you'll be a key part of the strategy team.

Critical to understanding the role of a Biz Dev person is first

 **Geek Note** In some companies, the business development folks are part of the fund-raising efforts, creating the business plan and presentations, and working with the venture capital community. Find out early on if that's part of your job; if it is, your role holds different challenges.

to know the company's background, plus the interest and expertise of its founders and leaders. For instance, if a bunch of techies have invented something and are running the show but don't have a clue about what to do next, you'll be an important decision driver. However, if the company is run by an old Internet hand with a full memory in his Palm Pilot, you may find yourself tagging along and taking notes.

Whether you're leading business development or you're just part of the team, it can get pretty frantic: As companies evolve, frequently changing direction midstream, Biz Dev must constantly correct the course, keeping the company on track. That may mean canceling or renegotiating deals you've already made (be careful not to burn any bridges or make enemies—it's a small industry, believe it or not).

You'll be expected to turn the business model into reality by finding and making deals with other companies. There are many steps to this process, from the initial investigating and research, to making the people connections (hope you like networking!) and negotiating the contract. You'll have to sweat every detail of this dance, including anticipating the "what ifs" of a very uncertain industry. Then you'll put the deal in place, which may involve a completely different set of skills.

Because things aren't always clear-cut, there may well be overlap between sales, marketing, content, and business development. For example, a software company may want to do a licensing deal with a big site; some firms call that "sales," but some place it under "business development." A major publishing site might need a yellow pages service. Is that content? Commerce? Business development? It may be that all three areas are involved in the deal to some extent, but the Biz Dev person will most likely be the one who pulls it all together.

Many specialties, like sales and marketing, have crossover potential for Biz Dev. One thing that definitely helps in this transition is some experience related to the content or subject matter of your firm. For instance, a music site would benefit from having a business development professional with a background in the radio, record, or music retailing industry.

You'll be expected to be flexible, versatile, and self-sufficient. If you're used to having a secretary or administrative assistant, forget it: You'll be addressing your own FedEx envelopes and putting together your own *PowerPoint* presentations. Your laptop may be your office, and you should be prepared to travel. But we know plenty of folks who limit their travel to a few conventions per year and do the rest by phone and e-mail. If you work for a big company, potential partners will probably come to you!

David vs. Goliath Issues

It does help to have some passing Internet experience to get hired into a Biz Dev position at either a David *or* a Goliath firm— but that's where the similarities end.

A David is especially hungry for alliances. You may well be the only hire in that department and have to make it up as you go along. There will likely be overlap between your activities and those of editorial, sales, and marketing, because many deals will affect those departments, too. Work closely with them to make sure all eyes are on the same prize.

With so many start-ups clamoring for attention, it can be tough doing business development for a David. No one has heard of you. You'll need to establish your credentials quickly and have done enough homework to have a pretty good idea of what you could do with prospective partners. If you're lucky, you might get your e-mail or phone call returned. Keep in mind your role in the negotiation (you're the party with less clout), but ask for what you and your company want, and take it from there.

If you work at a Goliath, your phone calls will most likely be returned—and quickly. With its established market presence, your firm will hold the upper hand in most negotiations—and it's always more fun to sit on *that* side of the table! When you get a deal in place, it can really make an impact on your company. That's the good news.

The bad news is you'll have less freedom to pursue your great ideas. We know one gal working at a large site who worked on only one or two content areas at a time—pretty tedious. And once you find the deals, the lawyers swarm and negotiations can bog down. Yawn.

Key Characteristics of Successful People in This Specialty

DEEP KNOWLEDGE OF THE INTERNET INDUSTRY

No one expects you to be a whiz kid on your first day, but your ongoing responsibility is to make sure that your company is making the right alliances and partnerships. You can't know that if you aren't always reaching out to see what the next big thing will be. Read the trade press voraciously; subscribe to every news-letter you can find. And, yes, they *will* pay you to just goof around the Web, because how else will you know what's really going on out there? You'll need to know who's doing what to whom and get updates every single day. You'll definitely need to differentiate between what seems like a viable idea and what won't fly; otherwise you'll be getting your company into all kinds of dead-end deals.

Biz Dev folks need a good handle on how Internet companies

work, the roles people take on, and how those things affect decision making. Let's say you've identified a potential partner: You phone the VP of business development, your counterpart at the other company. After one or two conversations, you realize the guy just fell off the turnip truck and can't get this done because the real decision maker is the CEO.

Structure and title aren't as important in the Internet game as who ultimately makes the call, so develop your sense of who the real players are by keeping up with the trades, asking a lot of questions, and listening to your gut.

GOOD PEOPLE PERSON

This position is all about relationships; if you can't relate to other people, you're dead in the water. You'll need to charm others into meetings they wouldn't otherwise take, then persuade them that your company and theirs can make beautiful music together. You'll need to be able to listen well, to understand what the other guy's goals are and work with him or her to figure out how to create a win-win deal.

The other part of the people thing is good relations with the internal team. Once you close a deal, you've got to get the folks who work with you to implement it; this includes putting up the new content, links, ads, and sponsorships—whatever the deal requires. And you may need to baby-sit them, because it can easily become an NIH (not invented here) problem; they're just not very enthusiastic about putting up something that they think they could have done better themselves.

STRATEGIC THINKER

We know one woman who was a master of all these areas, but had a bad habit of taking a meeting with almost anyone. The company she worked for had very specific goals and all these meetings weren't doing a thing to move the company any closer to them. Be realistic about what your firm is/does/can do and focus on the deals that can further its goals.

RESILIENT, BOUNCES BACK QUICKLY

Part of Biz Dev is coming up with more ideas and possible deals than are realistic. That's just part of the numbers game: If you throw enough things at the wall, something will stick. Some ideas won't be practical, others will be just plain dumb, which is okay, because you probably won't have the personal bandwidth to do everything you can think of. So when you come up with the Next Great Thing and it gets shot down (prepare yourself because this could happen in a very public way), pick yourself up, dust yourself off, and start all over again.

GOOD AT THE DETAILS

It's not hard to locate possible partners; the hard part is sweating the contract negotiations down to every possible deal point. Know what's really important and what you might be willing to give on. You may have to involve one or more layers of attorneys and higher-up management, so know your deal cold and how any number of scenarios will play out. (More on contract points in chapter 9.)

What to Expect Once You Start the Job

SOME MEDDLING BY UPPER MANAGEMENT . . . OR MAYBE NOT

Being a happy, productive Biz Dev executive at your company depends largely on how involved senior management wants to be and how comfortable you are with it. Will you be working with the founders on funding for the company? Try to get some perspective on this during the interview.

Sometimes the founder or CEO loves the cross-pollination that's part and parcel of working with other Internet firms. As the Biz Dev person, you'll be the clear number two and won't be setting much direction for your area. You may be the simple executor of your boss's deals (or worse, you're put in the role of the naysayer, pointing out to the boss that he or she is making silly deals).

On the other hand, sometimes senior management is too busy getting the site up or working out merchandising deals and is all too happy to leave the "relationship stuff" to you. Then you'll be in a position to help steer policy and strategy, leading the way toward alliances that make sense for the company.

NOT MUCH DIRECTION

It's rare that anyone will hand you a project or possible deal ready to go (and if they do, be suspicious—someone dropped it earlier on for a reason). Your job will be to sift through the random contacts someone else has made and the e-mails cramming your in-box every day in search of gems worth pursuing. More important, you'll be expected to be proactive in developing new relationships. You should be included in internal meetings where other employees discuss what's important, what they need, and where they want to go. Use those occasions to sniff out goals: it's not always as obvious as "Go locate a recipe finder for our site."

Don't Get Hung Up On

Trying to learn everything about a company and its goals before you start. The company will want to educate you anyway, so don't try to formulate a business development plan before you go to the first interview. You should however have some idea of what kind of companies you'd approach if you were in the job already. No doubt you'll be asked this question in the interview.

Biz Dev types aren't usually expected to know too much about the technology (of course, if you're going to work for a hardware or software company, you at least need to be trainable).

Don't worry if you don't know a lot of people in the business before you get started. It helps if you have some contacts, but the reality is the person you know at AOL is probably not the person you need to talk to anyway. Start networking immediately and you won't be at much of a disadvantage.

Typical Compensation

Business development is usually a well-paying area. There's your salary, plus the usual options and incentive packages; but you should also be able to negotiate additional rewards based on your performance.

The hard part, especially at a start-up, is that it's difficult to predict where your work will take you, so it's nearly impossible to determine beforehand a reasonable basis for an incentive program. This is where trust comes in: If you think the people you're going to work for are honorable, and you all agree what your job entails, begin by discussing a "range" for your future bonus. Once you get a feel for what you can do, propose a measurable standard for payment of that bonus. If you can get away with it, request quarterly payments: It ensures you're constantly adjusting the incentive plan to keep pace with the company's progress. Plus you'll collect your cash no matter what the fate of the company.

Interview Questions and Concerns to Be Prepared For

- What kind of work do you do now?

- Do you make deals?

- How much do you have to scout out the deals you make?

- Give me an example of a great deal you closed.

- How are you with contracts and negotiations?

- Have you attended conferences and conventions and made contacts there?

- What do you think of our Web site/business plan?

- What kinds of companies do you think we should be talking to?

- Have you ever managed an affiliation relationship before?

- How well do you work without supervision?

- How do you function within a team?

- What do you think of industry trends? (Could be anything . . . read up!)

- What sites do you think are doing a good job with partnerships?

- Can you think of any offline firms we should be talking to?

Get to Know

Everything! Business development spans every department in a company, so anything you can learn about the industry will help you do your job better. Biz Dev types frequently read everything they can get their hands on, even if it's not Internet related. Great business relationships can be made with brick-and-mortar companies, too. Be a sponge about trends happening in the real world, as well as in the Internet space.

A lot more general sites and organizations can be found in "Resources," but these Web sites are of specific use to business development.

- http://www.channelseven.com
Great *Narrowcast* newsletter.

- http://www.atnewyork.com
Good market intelligence on the industry, particularly New York–based companies; has a great newsletter everyone should subscribe to, no matter where they live.

- http://cyberatlas.internet.com
Good reference information on the industry, top Web site lists, and industry analysis; has the best demographics, basic industry info, plus specialized coverage (online financial, etc.).

- http://www.digitrends.net
This is the online site of a great magazine.

- http://www.bizreport.com
Digital business and e-commerce news; good newsletter.

- http://www.ecommercetimes.com
A must-read for Internet commerce, good for Biz Dev, too; in-depth interviews and profiles on the biggest players and trends; good archives and perspective.

- http://www.businessmarketing.com
B2B Internet ad and marketing news.

- http://www.iab.net/events/eventsource.html
Good list, by category, of various industry events.

- http://www.ad-guide.com
Good lists of resources, including Web marketing firms and
event listings.

- http://www.onlineinc.com
They host a conference called "Buying & Selling Content."

- http://www.internet.com
Has a conference called "Affiliate Solutions."

- http://www.refer-it.com
Clearinghouse of affiliate programs.

Deep Background

Every day, business development executives are coming up with
new and creative approaches to deal making, but the basic business relationships are the following:

Acquisition. Just like in the offline world, one company buys
another. Of course, Internet space complicates it greatly with issues like pooling of assets and goodwill.

Affiliation/affiliate networks. On the Web, affiliate networks let
smaller Web sites share revenue with larger sites by referring
traffic and sales to them. It's a way for the small-fry to get a share
in e-commerce revenues without selling anything directly.
LinkShare and Be Free are two of the biggest independent affiliate network organizations; by signing up with them, you can
participate in revenue-sharing programs in a few easy clicks. For
commerce sites, it gets you distribution with very little hassle.
The biggest sites like Amazon do their own independent affiliate

programs, crediting a small site with a percentage of sales sent through them.

Joint venture. When two (or more) companies launch a new business together. There are many variations on this theme, including which partner is the lead, where the company will be located, and how independently it will be run.

Licensing. A business relationship in which one party agrees to let the other use or share content or tools. Typically a monthly fee is associated with licensing.

Partnership. Can mean anything in Internet space, from a real joint ownership to a simple affiliation agreement. Get some clarity when you hear this one.

Syndication. Just like Ann Landers is syndicated to newspapers, specialized content can be created for the Web and then syndicated to multiple Web sites. Weather content is a good example. Revenue models vary by product offering and company.

NDA (nondisclosure agreement). A piece of paper that you will frequently be asked to sign at the beginning of a business meeting or negotiation. It means you won't tell anyone anything told to you about the company.

Where Can You Go from Here?

Business development is frequently a stepping-stone into senior management. It's a great place to showcase your strategic thinking and ability to carry out a plan. Because it's so much about relationships, the position is also very high profile. This cuts both ways, though: You're literally attaching your name and reputation to a company, so avoid working for one that you wouldn't go out on a limb for!

ALSO READ

Chapter 3: Sales
Chapter 6: Creative (for content ideas)
Chapter 7: Advertising and Marketing
Chapter 8: E-Commerce
Chapter 9: Some Specialties (law, etc.)

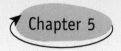

Chapter 5

OPERATIONS
Making It All Go

This might be the right place for you if your job right now is:

- Human resources
- Accounts receivable
- Accounts payable
- Controller
- Finance
- Operations

- Credit/collections
- Office manager
- Accounting systems
- Facilities manager
- Contract manager

Overview

At some Internet companies, the chief operating officer (COO) is more like a president; the Ops roles we discuss here are for those who handle more administrative areas. While everyone at your company is racing around trying to figure out how to turn what they do into a real business, the administrative staff has to treat it like a real business *today*. That includes making sure paychecks go out on time, handling payables and receivables, and getting the office cleaned every once in a while.

If you're already experienced in the finance, operations, or human resources department of a traditional company, most of what you know will transfer nicely to an Internet company. There are some exceptions, the biggest being—it is *not* business as usual. In the Internet game, it's far more critical to have a handle on what your company is all about, what their product or service is and who their customers are than at a traditional firm.

Here's an example: If you're the credit manager for a software company, many of your clients will be brand-new companies (meaning, high risk). What creative (and legal) ways will you find to extend them credit—and make sure you get paid? Turning customers down is very hard to do when the company is so anxious to make money, so the pressure will be on from sales and senior management to accept anyone who'll sign on the dotted line.

Another big adjustment: You may have to invent or adapt systems on the fly to get your work done. Remember that this Internet thing is still pretty new, with very few proven methods for doing anything! Don't forget what you already know about your old accounting software or credit collection methods, but take time to consider whether they're good enough for your new situation or if you need to buy, license, or develop your own methods for getting the work done.

The smooth functioning of an operations/administrative department is vital to the health of every company, but especially an Internet company. The company was most likely started by creative or technical types lacking the enthusiasm for the "boring" day-to-day details, so someone's got to hold it all together. For instance, hiring and retaining staff is crucial to a successful Internet venture, yet many companies start off without a thought given to human resources. As they grow, it becomes increasingly important to offer standard benefits like insurance, 401k accounts, flexible spending, and disability and maternity policies. There are also thorny legal issues like workers' comp and discrimination:

The operations person has to know when to call the lawyers (check out chapter 9 for more on law).

And then there are the unusual perks that are a distinctive part of the Internet industry—like Friday night beer blasts, free snacks and sodas at all times, and the company outing to the paintball park. Who's supposed to take care of all this? Take one guess . . .

The same thinking applies to financial and back-office management. Even companies not yet turning a profit need to pay their employees, establish bank accounts, do financial reporting, and have an accounts payable and receivable area. They still have to pay taxes and have their books audited.

Facilities and operations are crucial: Does the air-conditioning work in the summer, the heat in the winter? Are the T-1 lines backed up? Do the garbage bags on order actually fit the garbage cans? It may seem thankless (and it often is), but there isn't a company out there that can do without it.

What the Work Is Like

The following areas of responsibility may fall under this category. If you're pitching a COO job, be prepared to tackle all of this:

- Financial reporting
- Payroll
- Health insurance
- Dental insurance
- Vision insurance
- Short-term disability
- Long-term disability
- 401k plans
- Accounting
- Accounts receivable
- Accounts payable
- Credit and collection
- Working with outside auditors
- Less serious benefits
- Planning the office Christmas party
- Tax reporting

- Social security
- Unemployment
- Government regulations concerning almost anything
- Harassment policies
- Registering the corporation
- The IPO Roadshow
- Due diligence documents for a corporate sale
- Lease or purchase of a facility
- Facility maintenance
- Facility renovations
- Office furniture
- Telephone systems
- Purchase of hardware
- Purchase of software
- High-speed access
- Servers for hosting the Web site
- Server farm to host
- Backup and redundant lines
- Arranging access for remote workers

- Liability insurance
- Banking
- Investing excess revenues
- Foreign exchange (if operating in a foreign country)
- Postage meters
- Shipping and freight handling contracts
- Warehousing
- File management
- Equipment purchasing, leasing
- Office supplies
- Office management, including hiring and keeping a receptionist
- Setting HR policies
- Locks and security systems
- Choosing and supervising a company lawyer
- Private vs. public company issues, issuing stock certificates, etc.

As you can see, the administrative or operations area of a growing Internet company is something of a dumping ground: Anything to do with spending or collecting money, employment, and even equipment issues with computers, servers, and Internet access will end up at your door. You may also find yourself involved in finding office space for the company, an ongoing challenge in Internet business: Not only do you have to project the needs of a rapidly expanding company, but you'll be facing landlords who want lease commitments of several years. For a start-up, predicting the next six *months* is tricky, let alone three years! Some companies have taken to offering landlords stock options to get past the "risk" objections or to taking shelter under the roof of venture capital "incubators."[1] What guidelines will *you* have to work by in this area?

If you're at a small company, expect to see overworked producers straggle into your workspace (oh yeah, forget about having a private office) with some issues that are familiar and some that aren't. These may include rules about freelance talent, how to account for marketing expenses, or what contracts were signed for advertising.

An example: Tom Tech-Weenie forks over a handful of receipts from pizzas that were ordered over two weeks of late-night shifts. Is there a set expense form? Does it exist digitally? Can it be submitted digitally? Do receipts have to be originals, or can they be photocopies? How often should they be submitted? Do they need a manager's signature? When do checks get cut? Is there a petty cash account for future pizzas? Who controls its disbursement? You get the idea. In corporate America, the procedures were likely described in a handbook somewhere. In Internet space, *you're* the handbook—until you write it.

---

1. John Holusha, "Providing a Helping Hand to Internet Start-Ups," *The New York Times*, March 5, 2000, N.J. Real Estate, p. 9.

David vs. Goliath Issues

At a David, a COO (sometimes called controller, VP of finance, or VP of operations) may be an early hire ... and be the only one in the department for some time. This is a terrific opportunity for someone from a brick-and-mortar company because the issues aren't all that different: You'll be starting up systems and finding vendors to provide services. You can get hired right into a David without Internet experience, but be prepared to shoulder a large burden until the company grows big enough (or makes enough money) for you to hire more bodies.

For a Goliath, there are more hires for slots that parallel the offline world: accounting clerks, human resources staffers, etc. Office policy is likely to have already been established, so if you're a creature of habit, this might be a great way for you to break in to the Internet without toppling your sense of self.

At a Goliath company, your department is also probably the only one keeping anything resembling normal business hours. You'll be able to take advantage of the relaxed environment of the Internet industry, like dressing down. However, most Admin bosses still expect their staff to be at their desks by 9 A.M.

Key Characteristics of Successful People in This Specialty

EXCELLENT COMMAND OF YOUR SPECIALTY AREA

If you're going to contribute in a significant way to an Internet company, you need to know your work area *very* well. You can't be learning about financial statements on the fly when you're working with outside auditors. *Don't fake this.* If you're not experienced, you'll fall on your own credentials and it could be embarrassingly public. Admit what you don't know. If you're coming in as a COO, you'll need to be very well rounded to be able to handle all the responsibilities likely to fall under your umbrella.

ABILITY TO VIEW THE ENTIRE PROCESS AND YOUR ROLE IN IT AND TO WORK WITH OTHER DEPARTMENTS

Really figure out what your company is about, what the vision is, and how it's being carried out on a day-to-day basis. If you're the COO, make yourself an integral part of the organization and ensure that as new business is pursued and established, you understand how it needs to be managed.

EXPERIENCE WORKING WITH OUTSIDE VENDORS

It's the rare Internet company that doesn't rely on outside vendors for some essential administrative services, even if just for interim periods. If you've hired outside vendors for payroll services, accounting, auditing, benefits consulting, facility management, etc., you're a step ahead of the game. Know when the work requires a specialist and be able to source, hire, and manage that specialist.

With all the venture money flowing into dot-coms, the rest of the company may not be sensitive to spending issues. You'll be the one keeping an eye on where those dollars are actually going—which may mean being the grownup and saying "no" once in a while.

ABILITY TO INNOVATE SYSTEMS AND PROCEDURES

No one knows exactly what systems work best for an Internet company because it's all still too new. Are traditional accounting and financial software packages useful for reflecting the unusual nature of an Internet company and its revenue streams? Every person who handles the back end will need to make it work, and a senior operations person will be responsible for making sure that happens as the company evolves.

SET YOUR OWN PRIORITIES (BUT STAY FLEXIBLE)

It's likely you'll be given a tremendous amount of work to perform in an unrealistically short time frame (welcome to the Internet). And that's not counting the work that no one has even asked you to do, like redesigning the advertising department's invoices to reflect the information you need for billing records or creating a budgeting process for next year. You'll need to look three months, six months, one year down the road and prioritize, both for the benefit of the company . . . and for your own sanity!

What to Expect Once You Start the Job

A BUNCH OF WORK WAITING FOR YOU

If you're lucky, you'll find a desk, a computer, and a phone (if not, your first task is ordering them!). You'll most likely also find a big pile of stuff on that desk. The Admin area is rarely an early hire for an Internet firm, because it's a cash drain without an easily recognizable return to the bottom line. So anticipate that you'll face an enormous pile of undone (or badly done) work, which may include expenses owed to employees from months ago, contracts waiting for signatures, and who knows what else!

NOT MUCH IN COMMON WITH THE REST OF THE COMPANY

Let's be realistic: Most of the cool, creative types attracted to the Internet industry think your kind of work is Bo-Ring. They're a free-spirited, hardworking bunch but you can win them over, especially when they realize you're the one who gets them their paychecks on time and makes sure there's toilet paper in the bathrooms.

Try to withhold any disdain at their erratic work hours, less-than-buttoned-down attire, and eating habits (to them, pizza is one of the four basic food groups). Step away from the grindstone once in a while, join the weekly beer blast (even if you just have a soda), and you'll be fine.

NOT A LOT OF DIRECTION OR SUPERVISION

A COO gets a lot of work handed to him or her by top management, usually with little more direction than "Take care of this." The CEO likely wants to focus on the really fun part of running the company: the vision thing, strategy, conquering new markets, going public, speaking on industry panels. He or she *doesn't* want to worry about whether there's T-1 access to the new remote facility; but someone has to, and that "someone" is you. The COO must anticipate the needs of the company and solve problems before they're even on the radar.

Don't Get Hung Up On

Trying to become an Internet junkie. No one expects the Admin staff to be up on the latest cool sites. And although you should have some idea of what the company you're interviewing with does, no one will expect you to understand how the back-end works. They'll explain it to you when you start.

Typical Compensation

Most positions in administration and operations have job titles and pay structure similar to those of the offline world. The difference is that every Internet employee should be offered the company stock option package, which can pay off very big down the line (or not; see chapter 15).

Unlike most traditional workplaces, it's not unheard of for Ops staff at an Internet company to receive performance-based incentives. If specific goals can be set, you may be paid for accomplishing them. For instance, a new HR hire could get a predetermined sum once a 401k plan is set up. Or a controller might get a percentage of the operational costs he or she saved by negotiating a deal with an office-supply retailer. Show your ingenuity and gumption by proposing creative ways for your employer to reward you based on your ability to contribute to the company's goals.

Interview Questions and Concerns to Be Prepared For

- What is your current area of expertise?

- What does your current company do?

- What kinds of responsibilities do you bear in your current position?

- Are you comfortable taking on more responsibility?

- Have you ever supervised others?

- How big a staff are you used to working with?

- How hands-on have you been in your work, how much has been supervising?

- Have you ever hired employees to work with you?

- Have you ever hired and worked with outside contractors?

- Have you ever innovated/designed your own systems and processes?

- How do you feel about a formal vs. a casual work environment?

- How do you feel taking direction from younger, less-experienced people?

- Do you know anything about contracts and negotiations?

- Have you ever taken a company through a hyper-growth period?

- What do you do if someone gives you a project that you don't know how to tackle?

- What is your experience interacting with other departments?

- Give me an example of a situation in which you showed initiative and creativity in your job.

- What are your goals for yourself?

Get to Know

There are a lot more Web sites and organizations of interest in "Resources," but these are particularly useful for operations professionals:

- http://www.alleycatnews.com
News from New York's Silicon Alley; includes lots of information on start-ups and venture capitalists in New York City; good events, a CFO breakfast roundtable and summit, one of the few in the business.

- http://www.cio.com
CIO magazine online; usually meant for chief information officers, meaning the guys who order the computers, but not bad

for CFOs and operations types because they frequently have to worry about Internet access and servers, too.

- http://www.cfo.com
CFO magazine online; not exclusively focused on Internet stuff, but some good articles

- http://www.businessfinancemag.com/
Online resources for business finance professionals, some of which are relevant to Internet businesses, some not; choose accordingly.

Some good general small business sites:

- http://www.office.com

- http://www.bizzed.com

- http://www.business.com

Deep Background

Learn more about Internet business models. We explored the basic Internet business models in chapter 1. To be able to manage, or even participate in, the actual running of the company you'll need a much deeper understanding than you could possibly glean from our brief overview. There are articles in many current business and Internet publications that go into more detail about the economics of acquiring customers, back-end systems and costs, and how companies project forward to the time when profits might actually arrive. Stay current: There are developments by the hour that affect the business!

Understand how Internet companies book revenue. One of the most controversial issues in financial reporting for Internet companies is the issue of how they book revenues. Most e-commerce companies report all revenues on the top line, inflating their numbers because they haven't deducted the cost of the sale (and keep in mind that many e-commerce players are losing money, some of them a lot of it, to "own" that customer down the road).

A related controversy is how Internet content companies report barter. Most show it as revenue, when in fact, it's only unsold inventory they trade with other Internet companies so they won't have a blank space where ads are meant to run. Another accounting issue you'll reckon with is whether Web development costs are capitalized or expensed.

Get Up to Speed on the "Pooling" Issue

The world of Web mergers and acquisitions is profoundly affected by the FASB (Financial Accounting Standards Board) rulings on "pooling" and goodwill. Stay current on the latest.

There are clear accounting rules for revenue and they *must* be followed.

Where Can You Go from Here?

This is definitely a growth area for Internet companies. It shouldn't be a difficult lateral transition to make, but be choosy and pick a company whose business plan is solid and whose values and leaders you believe in.

Do it for a while at a medium level, like accounting. If you're good and willing to take on more responsibility, you'll go far, *fast*.

Do well as a COO at a start-up and you'll find yourself in very hot demand. Headhunters can't keep up with the demand for folks with this complex set of skills. Once you've done it successfully, you can write your own ticket: Go with a start-up and you'll command serious equity. Or go to a more established player and get home to eat dinner with your family a few nights a week.

One of our sources gave us a final piece of advice to pass on about this specialty: Make it a fun learning experience, and this job will be endlessly rewarding; make it a series of unbearable daily tasks, and it will eat you alive. By the way, our friend loves it!

ALSO READ

Read each of the specialty chapters, along with chapter 11 about working at a not-com.

Chapter 6

CREATIVE
Writers, Editors, and Designers Weave the Web

This might be the right place for you if your job right now is:

- Writer
- Reporter
- Researcher
- Editor

- Proofreader
- Graphic designer
- Art director
- Photographer

Overview

On the Internet, content is critical, even on sites that aren't really about the content. For example, it wouldn't be as much fun—or as easy—to find the right toy for that bratty nephew without the gift finder feature on a toys site. Music-buying sites would be downright boring without the latest gossip about Madonna; and whether they're selling tractors or mascara, e-commerce sites need something interesting to bring the customer back. This is the job of the creative group: making a site come to life. They're responsible for weaving together the various elements that make for a great end-user experience.

Creative types are truly at home on the Web, where they can be constantly innovating, finding new ways to deliver information and make it entertaining (or at least, look cool).

The possibilities for what can be done are increasing exponentially as technology progresses—so the creative department is one area where it's helpful to be just a little bit of a geek.

For example, an editor/producer needs to know the basics of HTML even if it's not a big part of their daily responsibilities. A graphic designer will be expected to be comfortable with online graphics and photo-manipulation software and have some working knowledge of HTML as well. Don't panic: There are plenty of books out there on HTML and crash courses that provide basic training over a weekend. Make this part of your homework.

What the Work Is Like

Before any site gets built, there are meetings—lots and lots of them. It's here where the brainstorming starts, white boards are filled, ideas are tossed back and forth, and mass quantities of pizza and Chinese food are consumed. At this early stage, it's all about collaboration, with everyone contributing, from the creative to the tech to the sales departments. Once the ideas begin to take shape, they're laid out in a "site map," which clearly illustrates exactly what happens when a visitor clicks on a certain icon or a page. At that point, the members of the creative team go to work on their individual assignments.

FOR WRITERS, EDITORS, AND PRODUCERS

At an Internet company, a writer/producer tends to do less writing than project managing.

As we just mentioned, creating a Web page or site first requires planning what will go into it: the actual copy, along with any searches, lists, polls, quizzes, photos, audio/video, forums, chats, links, and of course, commerce potential. The writer, editor, producer sees that those elements are created, organized, and posted to the site.

As for actual writing, think "short and sweet." Can you say it in bullet points instead of a paragraph? That's how people interact with their computer screen; and except for a few of the more literary sites, you won't find many long pieces on the Net. This raises an important point: If you've got a background as an investigative journalist and you really *love* doing in-depth pieces that require lengthy original reporting focusing on a single assignment at a time, trust us: *Don't* work for an Internet site. You'll hate it. One expert we spoke with said she's seen at least three people with this very background give it a try and then turn around and go back to the newspaper industry. Of course, not all newsie types hate the Web world: The leap is easier if you're a fact checker, sports reporter, restaurant or culture reviewer or editor, or if you rewrite wire copy.

And an increasing number of seasoned journalists are willing to take a crack at the Internet game, being lured to the dot-coms with promises of higher pay and those ever-present stock options. This trend is so significant that it's causing a serious brain drain in the print world.[1] If you've got the itch, just remember that writing for the Internet will require some adjustment.

The Web is an ever-evolving work in progress. Unlike print, your words may not stay the way you and God intended them for very long. A Biz Dev honcho may decide the tone is wrong; a client may not like your brilliant sense of humor (Cindy knows all about this one). Suddenly, your prose reads like a biology textbook. Learn to let go of your work or you'll be eternally frustrated.

---

1. Felicity Barringer and Alex Kuczynski, "Net Draining Talent from Print Media," *New York Times*, February 28, 2000, p. C1.

☞ SINATRA LIVES! (AT LEAST ON THE WEB)
Print vs. the Web

So how different is the Web from print? Here's an example.

Let's say someone gets the idea to do a tribute to the Chairman of the Board, Frank Sinatra. In the print world, a staff reporter for the newspaper or magazine would write a biographical story, then hand it off to the photo desk to find some images to accompany the article.

The Sinatra Shrine (http://www.nj.com/sinatra), on the other hand, is a living, breathing combination of biography, quizzes, audio and video clips, photos, and audience participation through forums, surveys and polls. The writer/producer envisioned and pulled together not just the print elements, but audio, video, and more, turning it into an eternal shrine people will visit for years to come, or at least until the site comes down. Meanwhile, the print reporter's story has long since hit the bottom of the birdcage.

An editorial position may also encompass the "community" or audience participation part of a site. Responsibilities may include creating and monitoring forums, discussion boards, and chats, anything that involves site users. These require a high level of comfort navigating your way around the Web, along with the ability to use Web-based forms and low-level HTML.

Let's talk technical requirements for a moment. For a writer/editor position, you'll need to know HTML—even though you

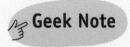 **Geek Note** Community positions are a great entry point for a Web career and can be performed remotely. See chapter 9 for a more complete description of community leaders.

may never use it on the job. Don't feel you have to be an expert before you apply, just be prepared to show you're conversant in the language and that you have a good idea of what can and can't be done with it. (Deborah admits that even after six-plus years in the Internet world she still hasn't learned HTML. She does, however, understand its possibilities and limitations.) According to some of our experts, it wouldn't hurt to become familiar with *Photoshop* either. No, you're not a designer—but this is a multimedia format, so get to know some of the tools that go into Web creation.

Those applying for a producer's job will need to be *very* good at HTML and to show work they've done. However, as a newcomer to the industry, you probably won't get hired into a producer's job straight off.

FOR GRAPHIC DESIGNERS, ILLUSTRATORS, ETC.

Even on the Internet, good design is still good design; but in some ways, the art of graphic design and illustration is dramatically different from its print world counterpart.

This is no longer a flat, two-dimensional world: We're talking multimedia, with pages that incorporate sound and animation, along with copy and illustration. You certainly don't have to know all of these things backward and forward, but you *do* have to be aware of how these elements affect your design.

Good news for those just entering the Web world: Even if you don't have Internet technical skills (yet), having an interest in things like photography, film, and music can be a help. These elements are enriching the online design world, beyond what's possible in print, so interests outside the standard design corral can evolve into useful skills.

Now for those technical skills: You can't fake it. If you're making the jump from an advertising agency to a Web design position, you'll need to know HTML basics just to get in the door. It's a layout tool; and as a designer, you need to understand your tools. You don't need to be a genius, but at the very least take a class or teach yourself by book (as one very successful Web designer we know did!).

Other standard tools include *Photoshop* and *Illustrator*. Investigate what they do, and play around with them. There are literally thousands of sites out there with great (and free) information about other cool design tools such as *Flash* and *Shockwave*. Again, don't worry about becoming a pro overnight; the technology changes so quickly it's impossible to be on top of it all. You'll "get it" once you start working with them on a regular basis. And don't forget what you know about print design: Web work frequently involves a print component for outside sales and promotional purposes.

This medium is about constant change. Your work doesn't end when you put up a site. It's more than likely that your colleagues will regularly want to change things you lovingly slaved over. If you have a hard time with anyone toying with your "vision," remember that there *is* no sacred ground. In this collaborative environment, your work is not yours exclusively. And just like our in-depth reporter friends, if you like taking your time on each piece and working on just one project at a time, take a pass right now on a Web career. You'll hate the demands on you, both technically and deadline-wise.

Like most areas of the Internet, your *passion* for the medium will go a long way toward getting you in the door, even if your technical knowledge is limited. Our source tells us, "I'm interested in someone who's *interested* in the Internet. You can be a great designer, but if you don't have a real passion for the Web, I'm not as likely to hire you. A lot of this is the unknown, so you have to have a certain optimism, like 'I don't know how we're going to do this, but I'll figure it out.' That's what I'm looking for."

David vs. Goliath Issues

FOR WRITER/EDITORS

A small start-up may be able to budget for only two or three content types, and it's unlikely that it will have an in-house production department to build the pages. Bottom line? If you go to work for a David, you'd better be versatile right from the get-go (i.e., you'll need to know how to produce what you actually write for the Web). Without production skills, you'll have a harder time getting hired. The company that interviews you will rightly think you need costly, time-consuming training—and may also suspect that as your skills develop you'll hold them up for a fat raise. Paranoia is a fact of life in the Web world!

FOR DESIGNERS

This is an area that's particularly easy to outsource, so it's unlikely a small start-up will spend money on an in-house art department. You'll find the most opportunities either at a small Web-only design firm or at a Goliath.

For both writers and designers, there are more jobs at Goliath companies. They're constantly hiring in these areas, and staffing new positions like fact checkers, proofreaders, copy editors, and researchers. These particular jobs often don't require anything other than familiarity with the Internet and are a great introduction to the world of Web content.

Designers may find that technical skills aren't as critical at a Goliath. Frequently, the company has sufficient staff to allow designers just to design, while tech stuff is left to programmers and site builders. Don't think this gets you off the hook, though—learn what you need to learn!

Whether you're interested in writing content or designing a site, a Goliath can afford to pay for training, and if you're good, you'll move through the ranks quickly. Take advantage of this and take the lead: If there's something in particular you want or need to become skilled at, ask for the training.

Goliaths frequently hire freelance writers and designers, particularly on one-off projects. Cindy got her start writing quick copy bits for various sites. Just having that Internet writing experience on her résumé opened the door for lots of other Web work.

Key Characteristics of Successful People in This Specialty

ABILITY TO THINK OUTSIDE THE BOX

The Internet isn't just a flat page of print. If you come from a print background and can't break out of that mold, you won't make it in the long run. The interactivity and the multimedia possibilities of this new medium require thinking that encompasses *all of it*.

WILLINGNESS TO GROW YOUR TECHNICAL SKILLS

Unless you're already an experienced Internet producer, no one expects you to have the ability to do all the technical stuff on day one. The same goes for designers and illustrators. But there *is* an expectation that you'll learn what you need to know (and quickly) without anyone holding your hand.

If you're sitting in a meeting and someone suggests using a *Flash* intro and you don't know what *Flash* can do, *ask* (after the meeting). Your colleagues will respect you for not trying to fake it. To create cutting-edge Web content, you need to keep up with technology and understand how it might work for you. The best way is to simply spend a lot of time on the Web, seeing what's out there and getting the vibe.

FLEXIBILITY ABOUT YOUR WORK AND JOB DESCRIPTION

This is our favorite theme for *all* job hiring areas in the Internet: We don't know of a single person hired for an Internet position who, within three months of signing on, was still doing the job he or she was hired to do.

For example, most publishing Web sites revise their content plan every quarter. Traffic on the Internet, and on a particular site, is quantifiable, so everyone knows pretty quickly whether a certain area of a site is sticky or not. When it's not, a staff writer/producer could be reassigned immediately to work on something different. Learn to swing with the punches. Even though you have a strong pride of ownership in what you were working on, there's usually a pretty good reason you were reassigned, so deal with it. And do it with a smile.

SELF-MOTIVATED, GOOD COMMUNICATOR

There's no time for baby-sitting in the Internet game, so you'd better be pretty good at structuring your workday, setting priorities, and being proactive in learning what you need to learn. If you're used to established checkpoints and deadlines, get unused to it: The Internet game is far more fluid. You were told you had until Friday to finish something, now you have until tomorrow. Learn to turn on a dime and restructure your to-do list on a regular basis.

Communication is also vital. Although this may be second nature to the writers in the crowd, designers take note: As part of a collaborative group, you'll need open lines of communication with your team and be able to educate clients who may not be all that familiar with Internet content and what it can do for them.

What to Expect Once You Start the Job

ENOUGH ROPE TO HANG YOURSELF

The management philosophy of most Internet firms: Throw people in the deep end and see if they can swim (swimming tips appear in chapter 16). It's not that they're malicious; Web types are just too busy to do anything else.

Ask for help if you need it. Admit what you don't know. Find your peers in the organization and get them on your side quickly to help you navigate the shoals of the unknown.

UNSTRUCTURED WORK ENVIRONMENT

Compared to a newspaper, magazine, or ad agency where deadlines may be (comparatively) more leisurely and work patterns more established, the Internet environment is chaotic. You'd be frantic too if you—or your client—had yet to turn a real profit!

Each company has its own approach to project management. In some places you'll have to be the evangelist, generating the excitement needed to get it off the whiteboard and onto the server. Other companies have systems and rules for getting things done. Find out the credo of your firm and make sure you're comfortable with it. Deborah, for instance, hates systems that pigeonhole work, but some people (like Cindy) crave orderly progression.

FOR WRITERS, FEW REPORTER'S PERKS

It can be a lot of fun being a print or broadcast reporter. An entertainment editor, for example, is used to getting invitations to movie premieres and restaurant openings. For the most part this gravy train has yet to arrive in the Internet world: You may have to beg to be put on press release distribution lists, much less be able to scam your way into classy events.

FOR DESIGNERS, ESPECIALLY VAGUE DIRECTION

The possibilities within Web design free the imagination. But they also make it tough to get concrete feedback from management or clients. Be prepared for some pretty fuzzy input ("I want it to look more, ummm . . . more 'tech-y' . . ."). This is assuming you get any input in the early stages at all. And be prepared to make changes . . . a lot of them.

Don't Get Hung Up On

LEARNING A PUBLISHING SYSTEM BEFORE YOU GET THE JOB

No one would expect you to understand theirs; they'll probably arrange formal training after you begin. This also applies, to some extent, to specific graphics tools for designers. Beyond knowing *Photoshop* and *Illustrator*, you won't be expected to be a whiz at their pet design tool right off the bat. Much of it you'll learn on the job.

BUILDING YOUR OWN WEB PAGE

For writers, having a personal Web page isn't necessary. For designers, however, it's a must. Our experts suggest building a simple Web site about *yourself*. It doesn't have to be flashy or complex, but having one will show you've given some thought to how your design ideas can work within the Web environment. And by all means, keep it current—there's nothing worse than a stale site.

Typical Compensation

We have good news for you: A competent writer, editor, or producer is a valuable commodity in the Internet world and can command a very fair pay package. Of course, the corresponding jobs in the print world have always been notoriously underpaid, so they're not hard to beat.

For designers, the salary at a Goliath firm will be comparable to that of a good agency. At a David, you may take a pay cut, but if you think of it as a paid internship where you'll gain valuable experience, it might not be so awful.

Expect a flat salary for most creative positions, because incentive pay doesn't make much sense here (we've heard of senior editorial positions that did get spiffs based on increasing traffic to the content on the site, but that's unlikely in your first Internet job). A good editorial person can move very quickly through the ranks, so don't worry if the salary you're first offered is on the low side. If you like the sound of it take it and prove what you can do. Then either ask for more money or move on.

You should be eligible for the company's stock option package plus any bonus or incentive plan that's offered.

Freelancers probably won't be paid as highly for an Internet gig as they would for an equivalent assignment for a magazine or newspaper, but freelancing for an established site will enable you to command better pay for future assignments . . . or a full-time position.

Interview Questions and Concerns to Be Prepared For

- How computer literate are you?

- Do you know HTML?

- What about *Photoshop* and *Illustrator*?

- Has your work been published on the Internet before?

- What is your favorite Web site?

- What is your idea of a good Web site? Give me some examples of sites you think are well put together.

- What is your idea of a bad Web site? Give me some examples of sites you think are poorly constructed.

- When you think about putting together a content section, what are your goals for the user experience?

- What do you think of high-tech gizmos on a Web site? (Have a good idea of what the philosophy of the company is before you answer this one . . . it may want the broadest possible user base and shun all bells and whistles.)

- What do you think of our Web site?

- What are your initial thoughts and ideas about what we could do to make our site better?

- What do you think of our competitors' Web sites?

- Tell me about an assignment you've taken on in the non-Internet world that showcases your creativity.

- How are you at managing projects?

- What about getting things done within an organization, particularly with people who don't report to you?

Get to Know

Besides the following, be sure to review the other listings in "Resources."

- http://webdeveloper.com
Good place for designers to get a feel for what's going on.

- http://www.content-exchange.com
Great site for writers.

- http://www.internet.com
Basic industry information on the front page.

- http://www.thestandard.com
Great general site.

- http://www.wired.com
Wired Magazine online, the granddaddy of them all; we like the calendar of e-vents and the "Current Hoo Ha," what people are talking about.

If you are interested in freelancing, check these out:

- http://www.guru.com
- http://www.elance.com
- http://www.wwwac.com

Deep Background

Lowest common denominator content. Sites that want a very broad audience appeal will usually set standards for what the design and editorial team must conform to, i.e., a not-quite-current version of a particular browser, no plug-ins required, etc.

Internet publishing systems. Most Web sites have two versions of their site running at all times: The development environment, where they build and test things, and the live environment, which is what an outside user sees. There are numerous publishing software packages that are used by the production group to post the approved new content to the live environment. *Story Server* and *Pantheon* are examples; AOL uses *Rainmaker*.

Site standards, templates, and rules. In the early days of the Internet, most content was utterly creative, governed by few standards or rules. Now, however, it's a very rare site that doesn't have (sometimes very strict) rules for how its content is displayed and what it can and can't do. Before you go to any interview, study your prospective employer's site in-depth to get a feel for what its rules of the road are.

Where Can You Go from Here?

Successful writer/producers usually progress up the food chain as either editors (the bosses of the other writer/producers) or into the technical area to become specialized producers. If you have a technical bent, you'll want to learn how to make the higher-order applications work. Then you'll *really* find yourself in demand.

It's also not unheard of for editorial types to make the transition into one of the business areas. You might join an interactive ad agency that builds commercial Web sites or do the creative on banner ads for an advertising agency. You could move into the business development area, creating partnerships with other Internet companies or syndicating your site's content elsewhere.

Similarly, designers can become creative directors, project managers, or even better, consultants (this is probably best for those who like the freelance lifestyle). Demand for consultants is growing as brick-and-mortar companies need help developing their Web look and strategy.

Once you've established yourself, your future in the Internet world can be as creative as *you* are!

ALSO READ

Chapter 3: Sales
Chapter 4: Business Development
Chapter 8: E-Commerce
Chapter 9: Some Specialties (community organizer)

Chapter 7

ADVERTISING AND MARKETING
Tow That Barge! Build That Brand!

This might be the right place for you if your job right now is:

ON THE AGENCY SIDE

- Account management
- Client management, development
- New business development

- Media planner and/or buyer
- Creative type (read chapter 6, too!)

ON THE CORPORATE SIDE

- Advertising management
- Marketing management
- Brand management
- Product Management

Overview

If you're a creative, outside-the-box thinker grounded in the basic principles of marketing and advertising, have we got a job for you! There's such a serious shortage of talent in this area, Internet companies are more than willing to take you on without Web experience, as long as you bring a strong marketing background with you. If, along with those fundamental skills, you bring the added benefit of understanding a specific business-to-business (B2B) or business-to-consumer (B2C) industry, you'll be golden.

The marketing of an Internet company is integral to its success. With so many sites out there, even the best of them will fail unless the marketers get the word out to customers. You might think of getting the word out in terms of expensive TV commercials (like the millions forked over by a few dot-coms for placement during the Super Bowl). However, there's a lot more to Internet marketing than blowing half your budget on a single TV ad. The best Internet marketers don't spend their big dollars like a drunken sailor. They carefully, methodically work *all* the options, frequently using the same media (like TV, print, and radio) that traditional companies use to build *their* brands.

David vs. Goliath Issues

There's even more good news for nongeeks in the marketing arena: You can pretty much choose where you want to work, because everyone from the smallest start-ups to the biggest In-

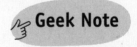 **Geek Note** Although this chapter focuses on marketing positions within Internet companies, don't forget traditional ad agencies that now cater to Internet companies: You can find a position in the Interactive division or go to one of the growing number of specialized interactive ad agencies that are springing up. In addition, any experience you have in a specific B2B vertical—say, auto parts or restaurant supplies—can help you land a lucrative Internet B2B marketing position within that category.

ternet behemoths are hiring marketers without previous Internet experience.

At a David, expect to be a one-person department into the foreseeable future. You'll be part of the senior management team, helping to build the Web site; making sure it appeals to your target market; creating the image, logo, and typeface. You'll probably order the stationery and business cards. You'll be building your brand from the ground up, supervising the creative staff, determining the media plan, and monitoring its effectiveness. You'll hire the PR agency (see chapter 9) or you'll do PR yourself. You'll come up with online advertising and promotion strategies, including how to get your site found on search engines. You'll plan and execute events and work with the content team on developing promotions. From the highest levels of strategy to licking the envelopes on a direct mail piece, this will be your domain. Sound good?

If it doesn't, consider working at a Goliath company, one with a more established presence and an existing marketing/advertising department. There you'll find positions closer in keeping with a traditional corporate structure. Perhaps you'll be in charge of buying media or doing promotions or sweepstakes. Not to say that the rules aren't different (don't even ask about the ins and outs of creating an online contest!), but your skill set will transfer with a minimum of hassle.

Key Characteristics of Successful People in This Specialty

SOLID EXPERIENCE WITH FUNDAMENTAL PRINCIPLES OF MARKETING

No one expects you to know the Internet inside out or your new employer's marketing philosophy on your first day of work, but they *do* expect you to know everything about advertising and marketing. You'll be the house expert and will need to do it all (or if not, find out how to do it quickly!).

LIKES A FAST-PACED, FREQUENTLY CHANGING ENVIRONMENT

The Internet world moves *fast*—and nowhere faster than in marketing, where a large percentage of the company's budget is dedicated to making a big splash very quickly. There are rarely months-long planning sessions. The drill goes more like this: Come up with your best guess, put it on paper, get it okayed by your boss, then run like crazy.

ABLE TO GO FROM BIG PICTURE TO MINUTE DETAILS IN A HEARTBEAT

A one-person marketing department, like the ones you'd find at Davids, needs to perform all the roles that a traditional marketing company divides into neat compartments: strategic planning, product development, market segmentation, brand building, creative supervision, media buying, monitoring, relationship and direct marketing, events, promotions, etc. You must have a vision of your company's brand and turn that into reality on an ongoing basis.

MULTITASKER

Again, you'll have to do it all—even more so than in other hiring areas. Can you juggle lots of projects and set priorities so you don't miss deadlines or crucial meetings? You'll have to.

GOOD COMMUNICATOR, WORKS WELL WITH OUTSIDE VENDORS AND THE INSIDE TEAM

You'll need to make your point of view clear to internal staff as well as manage outside vendors you're hiring for specific tasks.

If you're a lone wolf who doesn't work well with others, this could be tough.

OWN YOUR BRAND AND BE A FIERCE ADVOCATE FOR IT

You and the CEO/founder are directly responsible for ensuring that your image and message are communicated consistently to your targeted audience. The CEO might speak at conferences or be interviewed on CNBC, but you're the one who needs to bring the message and image to your customers.

What to Expect Once You Start the Job

What you'll face when you get started largely depends on where the company is in its life cycle. There are three likely scenarios:

Still in the conception stage.

Web site/product is built but there's no marketing yet.

Web site/product is built and marketing has started.

STAGE ONE

If you're lucky, you'll be in on the ground floor. You'll help clarify the company's target market and make sure the site or product appeals to those customers. You may help create the budget, deciding how much to spend on advertising. You'll be expected to work with the creative types on the look and design of the Web site and the logo, slogan, and messages for both online and offline media (like letterhead). You'll do the entire marketing plan, including the advertising you want to buy, planning seasonal campaigns, and choosing your media mix. You'll also have the fun of choosing the premiums the company gives out—the hats, T-shirts, whatever. You may get to hire an agency to help with creative needs and media buying. It's all wide open at this stage—which may be either exhilarating or a little overwhelming.

STAGE TWO

If the site or product is already built, the company probably doesn't want to hear what you have to say about its design or how customers will react to it—at least, not yet. The budget will probably already be set (at least until the next round of funding or the IPO). Your task at this point is to take what's already been created and build a brand around it, using the site/product and company as the building blocks. Your plate will be full of the same tasks outlined above, but you'll be picking them up at a different point. You may have inherited a bad logo or a mishmash of color schemes and typefaces; the founder may have already placed orders for ads or okayed barter arrangements that you consider less than ideal. Just pick it all up, run with it, and think about it as a test phase; you can change direction down the road after everyone's seen what works and what doesn't.

STAGE THREE

This is the stage most Goliaths are in. They've been around for a few years and are past launch. They have an image and a brand. The task here is to continue to build it, maintain its position in a crowded marketplace, and evolve from there. You must be creative and innovative plus very results oriented. When you first launch a site, you try a bunch of things, some of which work. Others don't. At this stage, however, you're learning from what's gone before and building on it. You're keenly aware of the competition and aren't counting on anyone to have done much analysis of the success of your marketing programs to date—you will likely have to initiate that yourself.

Here's what you'll face at all stages.

EXPECT TO BE THROWN IN FEET FIRST

This business is not for the faint of heart. You'll be in meetings on your first day, when you'll have no idea what's going on. Listen in and study up—fast. To be a functioning member of the team, you need to know everything that's happening in your company.

YOU'LL BE THE RESIDENT EXPERT ON ALL ISSUES MARKETING

Anything that relates even faintly to marketing will be thrown on your desk. You'll be dragged into a meeting about it during your first week and asked: What are the alternate methods of entry for an online sweepstakes? and Do you want to use the "http" as part of the URL on the brochure? Learn everything you can about online marketing as quickly as possible so you can be up to the task.

KNOW WHAT THE COMPETITION IS UP TO

Every day, make it a habit to check the Web sites of your competition. They're probably checking yours. As your company becomes more successful, it will be benchmarked against the leaders in the category. Stay on top of what they're doing—read all the digital newsletters and go to the conferences—so you can do it better.

BE YOUR OWN ADVOCATE

No one is going to be monitoring your workload or your ability to handle all the projects thrown your way. You need to know what you can and can't do and, where appropriate, make a case for hiring outside help. It's rare to find the budget set aside for outside creative design, media buying or PR: Make sure you can show your boss and the management team how much more efficient it would be to use outside specialists.

Don't Get Hung Up On

UNDERSTANDING ALL THE DETAILS OF ONLINE ADVERTISING . . .

Yes, it's likely that a big part of your job will be buying, supervising, and tracking the performance of online ad buys, which you may know nothing about. But don't make yourself crazy. If you understand the mechanics of buying other media, you can learn this, and one of your best sources will be the ad reps for the various sites trying to sell it to you.

. . . OR THE LINGO

There's a lot of detail in how online ads work: technical limitations, source materials, rich media, animation, etc. Your creative team will help you learn this.

Typical Compensation

As long as there are more openings for marketing executives at Internet companies than there are candidates for those openings, you're in the driver's seat. You should be able to command at least the same salary you made in the brick-and-mortar world, if not more. Then there are stock options, which could bring your compensation package to a very cozy place indeed.

The bonus or incentive portion of your pay will require some ingenuity. Believe us, your boss will *not* offer you the extra opportunity to earn more money or options: You'll need to initiate it—before you start, if possible. Once you understand what your responsibilities will be, ask for an incentive payoff based on achieving preset goals.

Here are some creative performance criteria:

- Percentage increase in traffic to the Web site.

- Number of advertising sales prospects brought in.

- Number of entrants to a sweepstakes (and, therefore, available for future direct marketing!).

- Number of subscribers to an e-mail list.

- Percentage of click-through on your advertising above and beyond the industry average.

Also, ask for regular three- to six-month reviews of the criteria to make sure they stay current. If you're doing your job and delivering on management's goals, the company will not begrudge paying you: You're a lifeline.

Interview Questions and Concerns to Be Prepared For

- What experience do you have in various aspects of marketing:
  Print advertising
  Radio and TV advertising
  Direct marketing
  Outdoor advertising
  Public relations
  Event planning, sponsorship, and management
  Sweepstakes and promotions
  Product placement

- Have you hired/worked with outside freelancers, creative talent, agencies, etc.?

- How much do you use the Internet?

- What do you like about the Internet?

- Why do you want to work at an Internet company?

- What sites do you visit?

- What do you like about those sites?

- What sites do you think do a good job marketing themselves?

- Which ones do a bad job, and why? What would you do better/differently?

- What offline companies do you think are the best marketers and why?

- What do you think of our site?

- Have you seen any of our ads/marketing?

- Who do you think our target market is?

- What might you do to reach more customers for our company/Web site?

- Give me an example of how you can juggle multiple projects successfully.

Get to Know

There are more general Web sites in "Rsources"; the following are of particular use to advertising/marketing types.

(Special thanks to Amy Harcourt of Definitive Marketing for her resource list!)

- http://www.thestandard.com
Great site for e-commerce information and Internet metrics.

- http://www.internet.com
Solid site for all things Internet; select "Internet Marketing."

- http://www.iab.net
The Internet Advertising Bureau.

- http://www.dmnews.com
A site devoted to direct marketing.

- http://www.fastcompany.com
Web site for the magazine *Fast Company*.

- http://www.business2.com
Web site for the magazine *Business 2.0*; focuses on the Internet-based economy.

- http://www.herring.com
Online edition of *Red Herring* magazine, covering the business of technology; go here to get the latest Internet news.

- http://www.zdnet.com
Technology news.

- http://www.davenetics.com

Daily e-mail newsletter that keeps Web professionals in the know.

Also check out:

- http://www.channelseven.com

Great *Narrowcast* newsletter; the Ad/Insight page is just for ad sales.

- http://www.adage.com

Ad sales and marketing types should be looking at this every day; "Interactive Daily" has the news on the Internet ad marketplace.

- http://cyberatlas.internet.com

Good reference information on the industry, top Web site lists, industry analysis; has the best demographics, basic industry info, plus specialized coverage (online financial, etc.).

- http://www.digitrends.net

This is the online site of a great magazine.

- http://www.businessmarketing.com

B2B Internet ad and marketing news.

- http://netb2b.com/

Net marketing, by Crain's, the same people who bring you *Ad Age*.

- http://www.iab.net/events/eventsource.html

Good list, by category, of various industry events.

- http://www.ad-guide.com

Good lists of resources, including Web marketing firms and event listings.

Deep Background

Branding vs. click through. As advertising on the Internet has evolved, the question of what you can accomplish with a banner or tile ad has remained an open-ended discussion. When you're the one placing the ad, you'd like to see actual clicks to it to prove people are seeing it and acting immediately. Click rates have fallen well below 1 percent as the Internet and its users become savvier. The other side of the coin (particularly if you're the one selling that online banner) is the substantial brand-building value of exposure; site visitors see the ad, even if there's no call to action and they don't click through to the advertiser's site. This debate is sure to rage on for some time.

Conversion rate. Once you get visitors to your site, what percentage of them do what you want them to do?

Database or e-mail marketing. The art of using your database as a sales tool: What do you send to the people on the list, how often, how do you manage that list in all its permutations? Direct mail marketing is an offline specialty that translates very well into Web applications. E-mail marketing has grown into its own sub-specialty of list management and messaging.

Loyalty programs. Covers a range of different reward programs given to Web visitors as incentive for desired behavior. Often supported by new Internet currency, like "beenz."

Permission marketing. Literally, asking a visitor's permission before you e-mail them with offers. You may ask them what kinds of things they'd like to hear about from you. The process is typically done by either an "Opt-In" or an "Opt-Out" box on a sign-up page: The default is almost always "yes."

Personalized or customized marketing. Conceptually, this means taking what you've learned about your customers based on their visits to your site, then reaching out to them with a message tailored to their interests. For instance, a regular visitor to the sports pages on your site would likely respond to an e-mail with information about a sweepstakes giving away tickets to his or her favorite team.

Reciprocal marketing. Glorified list sharing. One site agrees to send messages to their list for another or two sites swap lists for a marketing campaign. Obviously, cheaper than actually paying for a list, but may or may not violate your company's privacy guidelines.

Viral marketing. The mantra of Web marketing. Getting your users to market your site *for* you. The classic example is a free e-mail program, where every person who sends an e-mail is automatically advertising your service for you.

Where Can You Go from Here?

If you're an advertising or marketing star, the answer is . . . anywhere you want, and probably in a limo. You can easily advance to a senior management position at your own company, perhaps even the CEO job. You can move on to work with a bigger company, to an interactive agency, or even start your own company or consulting firm.

After some time spent as an Internet marketing "generalist," you may find there's one area you like best and want to specialize in. Go for it! As the industry grows, there's lots of room for someone with a successful track record to spin-off his or her own business.

ALSO READ

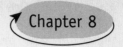

Chapter 8

E-COMMERCE
The Virtual *Ka-ching!*

This might be the right place for you if your job right now is:

- Buyer
- Merchandise manager
- Retail marketer
- Credit card marketer
- Direct marketer
- Retail analyst
- Cataloger

- Store or department management
- Customer service
- Credit manager
- Sales operations management
- Warehouse or fulfillment management

Overview

In its simplest form, e-commerce is selling things over the Internet. When most people think of online commerce, they think of B2C sales, like Amazon.com or STAPLES.com. These are the companies spending big bucks on TV and radio commercials, the ones that make the news or the covers of national magazines.

But don't ignore the *huge* e-commerce arena of B2B. As we mentioned earlier, these transactions range from auto body repair shops that buy and sell parts online, to highly sophisticated inventory and ordering systems for *Fortune* 100 manufacturing companies. It may not be as sexy as consumer sales, but this is a major growth area. Forrester Research predicts that B2B e-commerce dollars will jump from $43 billion in 1998 to close to *$1 trillion* by 2003.[1] This isn't just good news for those companies—it's *great* news for job seekers!

Companies conducting e-commerce can be divided into two basic camps: One is made up of established firms who use the Web as a new sales channel, aka clicks and mortars. Think of Nordstroms, Staples, Barnes and Noble, and Continental Airlines. With these firms, you can either click online or buy at their physical location.

The second camp is made up of companies that sell either exclusively or mainly over the Internet. Amazon.com, Cars Direct, and iPrint are examples of companies that didn't exist before the Web came into existence. They're known as "pure plays."

There's another "mini-camp" within e-commerce: content Web sites with one or two e-commerce specialists on staff to help them sell select merchandise of special interest to their visitors. The site that promotes a certain city might sell the jerseys of the local sports teams; a grief support site would make related books or videotapes available. Bottom line: No one wants to miss out on the opportunity to make money!

Although there are multitudes of job opportunities in all three camps, the newer companies may need you more. A start-up has to build everything from the ground up, including infrastructure; relationships with vendors; and, most important, a *customer* base. If you can bring specialized knowledge and established relationships to them, you'll be particularly valuable. Those who know how to sell are in great demand in the Internet; if you have retail,

---

1. Joanne Currue, "BTB: The Next Big Move in Online Advertising," *iMarketing News*, January 24, 2000, p. 30.

B2B sales, or merchandising experience, there are great opportunities awaiting you.

The Internet has created some unusual, as-yet-unproven methods for selling goods and services, methods that may eventually change the rules of retailing forever. From the buyer's standpoint, the Internet can be the "perfect" marketplace. Comparison shopping engines like mySimon.com search out the best prices for dozens of item categories. Then you have things like variable pricing, Dutch auctions, name-your-own-price sites, buying groups, and exchanges (definitions just ahead). This ultra-competitive pricing environment puts pressure on the merchant to offer a fabulous shopping experience—even if they can't always beat the other guy's prices. If the creative challenges of this new shopping frontier sound exciting and you're ready to turn the old ways of retailing upside down, read on!

What the Work Is Like

E-commerce encompasses *every* part of the sales process, so if we haven't driven this point home yet, get used to thinking beyond "your" particular duties. The following are some of the big issues e-commerce specialists must consider.

MERCHANDISE

What will you sell? Have you and/or the marketing department researched your target customers and their wants/needs? What are the price sensitivities? Who else is selling what at what prices? Which vendors will you work with? Are there issues with the vendor's channels or your parent company's other channels? Will you own the inventory or will you take orders and let the vendor fulfill them? Are you offering a wider selection of merchandise than that of real stores? What's your pricing strategy? How much inventory should you order? What arrangements/payments need to be made to secure inventory? How quickly will you turn over your "shelves"?

BUILDING THE ONLINE STORE

How will you organize your merchandise—by category or department? Will you require visitors to register before they can browse? Will you use focus groups to ensure the site is easy to use? Can you "personalize" the store for each customer? Will you display only merchandise that is currently available or will you take back orders? How can you convey your store's image through the Web site? Should there be specific content, like an article about ski weekends positioned next to the ski boots? Almost 76 percent of online shoppers say their purchase has been influenced by information they viewed at a site.[2] What will *your* accompanying content be?

ENABLING THE TRANSACTION AND PAYMENT

How will your shopping cart work? Will you buy the technology or build it yourself? How will the online registration process work? Will you save the customer's credit card and personal information? How will you guarantee the privacy of that information? Who'll handle getting you accreditation as a secure site? Which of these accreditation organizations do you want to use? Will you want your site rated by one of the ratings services? You'll need to set up online credit card transactions with banks and credit card authorizations. Policies and procedures will need to be established for handling both orders and returns. When it comes to order fulfillment, there must be processes for managing

---

2. Kenneth Hein, "Online Content Changing Buying Methods, *iMarketing News*, January 31, 2000, p. 1.

order flow, reporting on activity, and dynamic reporting of merchandise availability.

CUSTOMER COMMUNICATION AND SERVICE

How will you confirm orders and send communications back to the customer? Will someone follow up on customer satisfaction? How? Will your company take inquiries and credit cards over the phone? Will there be live customer support chat available? At what hours? Who will staff it? Will you outsource it? How will you handle returns? In this area, click and mortars have a huge advantage: Customers who know they can return an online purchase at the mall are much more willing to buy. This has led to a trend toward "outsourcing" the returns function: In some shopping malls, you'll find a kiosk that handles returns for multiple Internet merchants. These are just a handful of issues surrounding customer service, an area that is so critical to e-commerce that it's quickly becoming its own specialty.

HANDLING THE "STUFF"

There will probably be a need to create a warehouse, organize its operations, plus hire and manage workers for that facility. Someone has to make arrangements with shipping companies and packaging manufacturers. Successful e-commerce requires implementation of automated systems and feedback into the Web site to automatically update order information and tracking.

CUSTOMER ACQUISITION AND RETENTION

Once you've sold something to someone, how do you manage the relationship with him or her? How often do you contact the customer, and with what messages? Will you outsource the handling of the e-mail messaging? How can you customize visits to your site to make it a more satisfying experience for customers—and translate that into additional sales?

And how do you identify your target market and reach out to new customers? How do you make sure they're qualified prospects, not just numbers? You'll have to work with the advertising and marketing staff to create promotions or coupons, as well as pursue affiliate programs that will feature your store in more and more places.

BUSINESS ANALYSIS

What percentage of visitors who come to the site actually buy something (conversion rate)? What are they buying, when are they buying it, what items are they buying together? Are they abandoning your shopping cart because your process is too complicated? Are they repeat visitors or are they shopping with you just this once because of a special offer? How do your metrics compare to the industry standards and those of your direct competitors? Frequently, investors and shareholders demand these figures as one way to measure you against others in the market. To make it, you'll have to keep one eye on your key numbers and course-correct as needed.

Okay, take a breath now—but remember that *all* of these areas need to be deftly handled if an e-commerce effort is really going to fly. In some cases, one person may do all of them (yikes!), but even at a well-staffed Goliath, you'll be required to pitch in whenever it's necessary. And if that's not enough balls to keep in the air, working in e-commerce also means researching new systems to streamline the process and seamlessly integrating them into the company.

David vs. Goliath Issues

If you're considering e-commerce, think hard about how you want to spend your workdays, because in this area, the David vs. Goliath differences can be more pronounced than almost anywhere else in the Internet.

At either kind of company, the first thing to ask is: Are they an e-commerce company or does the bulk of their revenue stream in from elsewhere? This can affect the firm tremendously—to say nothing of your future. After all, if they've put all their eggs into the e-commerce basket, you'll want to know that *someone* at the firm knows the category and how to sell things over the Web.

Another key factor to consider is whether the company is simply developing a new sales channel or creating something brand new. If your prospective company is a multi-million-dollar retailer, for example, but it's planning on only a two-person Internet group, you've got to question its commitment to the whole venture. (**Note:** If you're helping a brick-and-mortar company launch itself onto the Internet, we suggest you read chapter 11 about working at a not-com.)

At a pure-play David, you could be part of a one- or two-person team responsible for everything from picking the merchandise to packing the orders. If the site takes off quickly, you'll need to get all hands on deck to help. If you're willing to roll up your sleeves and learn a lot very fast, this can be a priceless experience.

At a Goliath, your role will probably be more defined: Perhaps you'll be the buyer/merchandiser for a big site, but focused on a single category such as toys or clothes. There will be a lot more structure; you probably won't have to do the count at inventory time or run the analysis of abandoned electronic shopping carts. If you're one who needs a little more organization in your life, this might be the better choice for your first Internet gig.

Key Characteristics of Successful People in This Specialty

ABLE TO MOVE FAST

Don't make the mistake of equating e-commerce with traditional retailing. A clothing store in a mall, for example, may introduce new lines of apparel just a few times a year. In the e-commerce game, things move fast and you need to respond in kind. If your customers tell you they're looking for something that you don't stock, you'll need to source it and offer it ASAP.

FAMILIARITY WITH NUMBERS AND REPORTS

In the quantifiable universe of the Web, you'll quickly find out if something is selling or not, whether your customer service department has a backlog of complaints, or if customers are balking at your shipping and handling charges. All that information *can* be extracted, but if you're numbers-phobic, this will be a tough part of the job.

ADAPTABLE AND COMFORTABLE WITH CHANGE

Just like the other job specialties we discuss in this book, an e-commerce position is ever changing. What you *think* you were hired to do might not be what you end up doing. The most successful e-commerce specialists are versatile and can roll with the punches.

DEVOTED TO THE CUSTOMER

The key to winning the e-commerce game is understanding *everything* about your customers: who they are, how often they visit your site, what they look at, what they buy, whether they respond to discounting. Amazon is the prime example of an e-commerce company that grasped this concept early on and is expanding their categories all the time. Owning a *lifelong relationship* with the customer is the main goal of e-commerce. If you want to win, learn to work the available data to continually improve customer relations. Think like a customer. Never take your eye off this goal.

KEEPING UP WITH TRENDS

Like everything else in the Internet, e-commerce is changing rapidly. Even if the general news in the Internet industry doesn't appear to affect your daily work existence, keep up with the trends, specifically what others in your segment are doing. Who's offering free shipping and what's it costing them? Who's buying what company and how will that affect their overall strategy? Which companies went under and why? Read everything you can about Internet business in general and e-commerce in particular and know what's happening in your vertical, both online and offline.

TEAM PLAYER

Put away the cape, Superman (or woman)—you can't do it all yourself. A successful e-merchant needs marketers to help acquire customers, the creative group to make the site exciting, programmers to make it work, and the admin and tech staffs to ensure reliable performance. You'll be working with everyone. Even if you're not their boss, you need to know how to best capture and hold the attention of others on the team long enough to get your job done.

What to Expect Once You Start the Job

This depends on the kind of company you work for. Is it a brick-and-mortar retailer breaking into the Internet as a new sales channel? Is it a small start-up in specialized industrial sales? Is it a cybermall trying to cover many categories? Where you work will largely determine the intensity levels of the following.

JUMP HEAD-FIRST INTO THE TECHNOLOGY

Even if you know a lot about selling, you're not likely to know very much about online credit card authorization, secure servers, online order processing, or live chat for customer service. Again, you don't have to be a geek, but you must be able to talk the talk. Spend as much time as possible with the techies and learn what you need to know to do your job.

BENCHMARKING AGAINST OTHER E-COMMERCE SITES

The world of Internet commerce changes fast, and you'll be expected to know what other sites are up to. Your direct competitors' sites should be on your radar every day: Are they offering discounts, coupons, free shipping? Where did they show in the ratings last month? At any given moment, be prepared to talk about what others are doing and what your response to their moves should be.

DATA, DATA, DATA

Good consumer data is the currency of the Internet. Most companies spend far more to get a customer than that customer spends in a single visit. However, the company is investing in the *lifetime* value of the relationship with that individual.

The increasing precision of customer-data mining is staggering: You can determine the number of visitors to a site, what shopping carts are abandoned, which areas of the "store" have been visited, what combinations of merchandise are being purchased, average order sizes, preferred shipping methods, and geographic information. You can even monitor the performance of your customer service operation. One of your biggest challenges will be finding the time to get familiar with these numbers. Ask for the actual reports or access to online reporting systems and learn to make sense of the numbers. It's absolutely crucial to making your business successful.

PRESSURE TO SUCCEED . . . QUICKLY

An e-commerce pure play has to prove itself pretty much out of the chute if it's going to survive. The marketing department will throw a lot of money at potential customers, tempting them to your site, so when they get there, you gotta give 'em a great shopping experience that encourages them to come back again and again (thus justifying the dollars spent to acquire them). You need to hit the ground running.

Don't Get Hung Up On

UNDERSTANDING BACK-END SYSTEMS

Someone will explain this to you.

CREDIT CARD SECURITY AND PRIVACY ISSUES

There are technical people to handle this end of things, although you should be current on the latest issues surrounding it. Read the trades.

Typical Compensation

There's good news for e-commerce executives: Because traditional retail management has historically paid so poorly (compared to other industries), you'll do fine in the Internet world. Expect a fair salary—then the negotiations begin. You should get stock options (read more about this in chapter 15) and a performance component included in your pay package.

It's probably not reasonable to expect a percentage of sales (why would they want to give their revenues to you?) based on performance, but it *is* reasonable to ask for a quarterly or half yearly review with a bonus tied to specific, attainable goals. For instance, as a merchant, if you successfully add a new category by a certain date, you could ask for a set amount tied to that goal. Or if you're responsible for setting up a new warehouse system, request a fair cash bonus or additional options upon completion. If the company hands out end-of-year bonuses based on performance, make sure your employment letter includes that as well.

If you're considering working in the e-commerce department of a brick-and-mortar company, remember that your compensation will probably be close to what your non-Internet counterparts are making. It's unlikely that you'll be granted an "Internet salary." But if it's a good stepping-stone, start there, learn everything you can, then go to a pure play and get paid a premium for all that great experience!

Interview Questions and Concerns to Be Prepared For

- What e-commerce Web sites have you bought from?

- What e-commerce Web sites do you think are good? Why?

- Which ones do you think fall short? Why?

- What would you do differently on the bad ones?

- Why do you want to be in the Internet business?

- Current e-commerce issues and deals: What do you think of them?

- How does what you do on a daily basis translate into the Internet?

- Do you have a Rolodex of contacts in our category?

- Specific questions related to the vertical category and offline players in the same category.

- What bad business decisions have you made, and what did you learn from them?

Get to Know

Besides the following, be sure to review the other listings in "Resources."

- http://www.xceedintelligence.com/
Research company on e-commerce; free reports plus stuff you can pay for.

- http://www.internet.com
Basic industry information on the front page.

- http://www.bizreport.com
Digital business and e-commerce news; good newsletter.

- http://www.ecommercetimes.com/
A must-read for Internet commerce, good for Biz Dev, too; in-depth interviews and profiles on the biggest players and trends; good archives and perspective.

- http://www.e-businessworld.com/
Good for e-commerce; has a newsletter.

- http://www.iab.net/events/eventsource.html
Good list, by category, of various industry events.

- http://www.ad-guide.com/
Good lists of resources, including Web marketing firms and
events listings.

- http://www.dmnews.com
A site devoted to direct marketing.

- www.iconocast.com
One of our favorites; great industry analysis, inside gossip
(sometimes *so* inside, no one but the guy who writes it understands it!); the weekly newsletter is a must-read.

- http://www.jup.com
Jupiter Media Metrix Communications Web site; a major research firm; posts interesting articles, plus information about
its seminars and trade shows.

- http://www.forrester.com
Another big Internet research firm; interesting snippets from
its reports and studies, plus info on its seminars.

- http://www.atnewyork.com
Good market intelligence on the industry, particularly New
York–based companies; has a great newsletter everyone should
subscribe to, no matter where they live.

Deep Background

Affiliation/affiliate networks. On the Web, affiliate networks let
smaller Web sites share revenue with larger sites by referring
traffic and sales to them. It's a way for the small-fry to get a
share in e-commerce revenues without selling anything directly.
LinkShare and Be Free are two of the biggest independent

affiliate-network organizations. By signing up with them, you can participate in revenue-sharing programs in a few easy clicks. Commerce sites can establish distribution with very little hassle. The biggest sites—like Amazon—do their own independent affiliate programs, crediting a small site with a percentage of sales sent through them.

Auctions. Just like their offline cousins, online auction sites sell things to winning bidders. eBay is the biggest site of this kind, but there are numerous specialty sites, B2B sites, and many variations on the auction model, including reserve price, Dutch auctions, and private auctions. Many retail sites are adding auction functionality for certain items or categories; online classifieds sites use them to add fuller features to their traditional listings.

Buying groups. An interesting twist on the idea of bulk discount: Web users agree to participate in a buying group for a specific product. If enough people join in, the seller lowers the price for all. They make it challenging to figure out how to compete against them if your site sells the same products.

Commerce and content. The idea here is to put relevant content next to stuff that you're selling, offering a better user experience and—you hope—resulting in more sales. An e-commerce site selling wine might offer a primer on wine tasting or information about various vineyards, thereby encouraging imbibing.

Comparison shopping engines. Users choose an item to shop for; the comparison engine searches the Internet for the best price.

Dynamic pricing. One of the great innovations of the Internet. The price of a product or service can change based on any number of factors. There's never a dull moment if you're the one trying to figure out how to set prices.

Exchanges. A big trend in B2B e-commerce; buyers and sellers of almost anything meet and agree on a price for the product. This can make industrial buying and selling much more efficient, because it provides exact information about product availability and pricing to all the players, not just the biggest ones or the more geographically desirable.

E-Mail marketing. Reaching out to your users/buyers via e-mail with additional information and/or offers. See details on the variations in chapter 7.

Personalization. Creating an individualized experience for all visitors of your Web site. This may include greeting them by name, showing them merchandise similar to what they've bought before or accessories to enhance their purchases. Encompasses e-mail marketing, too.

Portal placement. An exclusive deal for key placement with one of the big portal players who has a lot of traffic within its site. This almost always costs a lot of money (which may or may not be justified in terms of the cost per acquired customer), but it gets you good visibility, squeezes out your competition, and can jump-start your traffic and sales. (See also "Anchor tenant" on p. 32.)

Revenue sharing. Just like it sounds: sharing the cash. Generally refers either to deals you make through an affiliate network (see above) or to individual deals with other sites that bring prospects to yours.

Where Can You Go from Here?

Once you've mastered e-commerce, the Internet world is your oyster. You can rise into a management position at the company you've helped build: If you've been part of the core team that helped the company grow, you'll be rewarded with more responsibility (and, you hope, more money).

Perhaps you'd like to strike out on your own as a consultant, maybe even start your own e-commerce company? Once you've done the e-commerce dance, you can apply those valuable, hard-earned lessons to other categories or services. It's yours for the taking.

ALSO READ

Chapter 3: Sales
Chapter 4: Business Development
Chapter 6: Creative
Chapter 7: Advertising and Marketing

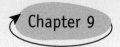

SOME SPECIALTIES
Law, Public Relations, Community

As we researched this book, we uncovered three areas of Internet business that demanded extra attention. They are law, public relations, and a new specialty—the Web site community organizer. They aren't *quite* large enough to warrant their own chapters, but they *are* bigger than a bread box, so we've grouped them together.

LAW
THE PARTY OF THE FIRST PART . . .

This might be the place for you if your job right now is:

Anyone with a law degree is a potential candidate to work as an attorney at an Internet company, but the following chart reveals which are the best (and worst) fits for making the transition:

GOOD	NOT SO GOOD	A BIG MAYBE
Contract/transactions	Real estate	General practice
Corporate (larger companies)	Tax	
Intellectual property	Estate and probate	
Media/entertainment	Labor	
Small business	Immigration	
High-tech corporate	Criminal trial law	
	Family	
	Personal injury	

Overview

If you want to try this Internet law thang, let's start by differentiating between (1) cyberlaw, (2) being an attorney at an Internet company, and (3) working for a firm with an Internet practice.

Cyberlaw encompasses the sexy, groundbreaking decisions that help define the law within emerging technologies. It may sound like exciting courtroom drama, but the bulk of practitioners of Internet law are generally not heavily involved in prosecuting these cases. It costs money to bring such lawsuits and most are usually settled.

The demand in the Internet business world is for lawyers practicing within an Internet company or as outside counsel, or working in a traditional law firm with an Internet practice or one that specializes in Internet law.

As with any small- to medium-sized company, a staff attorney at an Internet firm needs to juggle a wide variety of legal work— and at blinding speed. They must also have a pretty good understanding of the technology, such as whether an outsourced application will be problematic with the use of various browsers or if the audio is streaming or coming from sound files. Issues like these can and sometimes do have legal implications.

Like most law jobs, your workload will be very intense, but

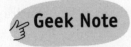 **Geek Note** What if you don't have a law degree (for instance, you're a paralegal or legal secretary) or you've got the degree, but don't want to use it anymore? Try business development (chapter 4)! A paralegal could be a crackerjack deal closer, contract administrator, or syndication person. A lawyer could move over to Biz Dev and break out of the mold—and away from all those lawyer jokes.

you'll get to handle several different projects and wear a couple of hats, which can make for a stimulating workweek. Below is a list of the kinds of issues and documents that could thump onto your desk on any given day:

- Nondisclosure agreements
- Intellectual property licensing
- Privacy policies and terms of use
- Copyright, trademark, and patent (intellectual property)
- Co-branding agreements
- Revenue sharing
- Consulting and work-for-hire agreements
- Property leasing
- Stock offerings (infrequent)
- Mergers and acquisitions (infrequent)
- Content licensing and syndication
- Employment law
- SEC filings (infrequent)
- Due diligence documents for sale of company (infrequent)
- Incorporation documents
- Shareholder issues
- Employee stock option plan
- Strategic partnerships

- Advertising, sponsorship, and media-placement contracts

- Hardware and software purchase and lease contracts

- Web-hosting agreements

- e-Commerce tax issues (infrequent, if ever—mostly theoretical now)

- Sweepstakes rules

- Giveaway rules

- Domain name disputes

What the Work Is Like

If a company is growing fast enough to hire a full-time attorney, you can bet there's going to be a lot of work. It's likely they expect not only your legal expertise but also your take on other business decisions, such as Biz Dev deals. Frequently, you'll be the *only* lawyer involved in a deal; to foster good relationships in this business, you'll need to act for the benefit of both your company and, to some extent, the other party.

To be most effective, educate yourself. First, learn how your company (or client) is making money. What's the business all about? Review the various Internet business models in chapter 1. Learn as much as you can about the various areas within your company. Are they content driven? This means focusing on licensing and intellectual property ownership issues. Do they sell software? Software licensing and technology contracting with an eye to future innovations are of paramount importance. Are they an e-commerce site? Transactional contracting will be top of the list. Set priorities and decide which contracts to spend most of your time on. Also, take time to figure out how much clout your company has: You need to know how much negotiating muscle you'll have.

Next, learn about the technology that makes the business go, from the hosting to the software and hardware that runs the Web site. You won't be able to make intelligent legal judgments about these vendors and their agreements unless you understand how it all fits together.

The Internet business doesn't offer the luxury of time. You'll be expected to cut to the chase and make sure that the legal details are solid enough to make deals work. As one source told us, "It moves about a hundred times faster than normal legal procedure!" There isn't time for fourteen drafts of the same contract or the refined and elegant legal language you may cherish: Just get it done. Accept the fact that it won't ever be perfect; frequently, you'll have to make sure you've covered the greatest areas of potential liability that let the business move forward. Internet deals happen in a very short time frame, so if you don't keep up, the company may very well go ahead and do it without your okay—even if it could be costly down the road.

As the in-house attorney, use outside counsel judiciously: It can get very expensive, so you'll want to take on as much as you can before you consider sending work out. Narrow issues surrounding a particular contract down to what you *really* need, and get it all

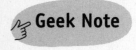 **Geek Note**   Only very rarely does an Internet dispute make it to court, largely because doing so is expensive and frequently the issues are moot by the time the trial begins.

done in a single negotiating session. You may also want counsel to draw up initial documents and contract templates for strategic reuse.

Very often, the attorney takes on the role of killjoy. You'll have to put the brakes on lame deals that don't make sense, are too vague and nonbinding, or create excessive liability exposure. This is particularly true when dealing with younger Biz Dev types and advertising account executives who don't possess much experience. As one source describes it, "You've got to let them do business, but you have to save them from the suicide missions." Protect your company to the best of your ability, take a deep cleansing breath, and pick up the next contract on the pile.

For an attorney coming from the wood-paneled, leather-bound environs of a traditional legal firm, the culture of the Internet world is a big shock. Avoid being branded a stiff before you even start: Call before the interview to ask if you should or shouldn't wear a suit. The answer will usually be to dress casually. And no matter how lofty your law credentials or prestigious your background, stay humble. You don't really know their business (yet) and will accomplish much more if you lose the attitude and ask a lot of questions instead.

In other areas of corporate culture, you'll be asked to work on complicated, sometimes confidential issues while sitting in a public work area with no window, no door, and no secretary. You'll be expected to redline your own documents (learn *Word* if you don't know it already), send documents via e-mail instead of FedEx, answer your own phone, and send your own faxes. Again, no complaining—you wanted to leave the old world for the new world of the Internet. Welcome to it.

David vs. Goliath Issues

Unless you're joining as both the general counsel and VP of business development, a lawyer won't be one of the first hires at an Internet start-up. If you *do* get hired into a David, you'll need to be a crackerjack generalist from day one and know the Internet space really, really well.

A bigger, more established firm with one or more attorneys already on staff can afford to give you some time before you merge into the Internet fast lane. If you bring some specialized expertise to the job, like mergers and acquisitions, and your Goliath employer is in the midst of acquiring smaller fish, the transition may be very smooth. Bottom line: If you're convinced you want to try your hand at a start-up, cut your teeth at a big Internet firm for about a year, where you'll deal with a combination of new media, transactional, and corporate work.

Don't Get Hung Up On

DETAILS OF FAMOUS CYBER-LAW CASES
No one will ask you about them, except maybe at a cocktail party.

Typical Compensation

If this amped-up version of law practice sounds thrilling, great. But first, slow down long enough to review the financial implications: If you've been practicing corporate law (particularly for a big-name firm), Internet staff salaries are going to disappoint you. If you've been doing general practice or working as a staff attorney at a corporation, the shift won't be as devastating—the Internet practices of the major firms or Internet specialty firms might be more in line with what you're used to.

The heartening news is that as with most Internet companies, you have a chance to share in the company's success. Stock options are a standard part of most Internet pay packages (read chapter 15 for more details—but you probably already know how to decode the options legalese, don't you?). Make sure you understand what stage the company is in before you get those options so you're clear on the potential upside.

An attorney at a start-up should also be eligible for annual bonuses based on both individual and company performance. It's not easy thinking of ways to provide incentives for a lawyer ("Finish ten deals this week and I'll pay you a grand!"), but if you're creative and motivated, an open-minded CEO might be willing to negotiate something.

Interview Questions and Concerns to Be Prepared For

- Have you done any dot-com work before? What specifically?

- What do you think are critical and common legal issues in this industry?

- How familiar are you with the Internet and Internet technologies?

- How much time do you spend on the Net?

- What sites do you visit?

- Are you familiar with Internet privacy issues?

- Have you done intellectual property work?

- Do you know how to transfer a domain name?

- Do you know how to do an online trademark or patent search?

- What do you know about_____law? (See preceding list to fill in the blank.)

- How good are you with emerging technologies?

- Can you juggle many projects and set your own priorities?

- Are you a good people person?

- Are you a fast worker?

- Can you deal with the thought that your work will contain some loose ends?

Get to Know

You'll find many more general Internet sites in "Resources," but here are some that are more law-specific:

- http://www.internetlawyer.com
Features research, news, and information for the legal profession; great tutorial on Internet law issues.

- http://www.thelawjournal.com
Wide variety of legal resources and information for legal professionals and those just interested in law.

- http://www.findlaw.com
Comprehensive portal with links to sites ranging from law schools to federal regs to legal cases.

- http://www.gigalaw.com
Legal info for Internet professionals.

- http://www.law.com
Excellent general resource for lawyers.

Where Can You Go from Here?

A competent staff attorney at a growing Internet firm will become an increasingly important part of the senior management team. We've heard of Internet attorneys going on to run business development or step into COO or president roles.

As companies progress through their life cycles, corporate counsel's responsibilities will change; if you're the first lawyer hired at a start-up, you may find yourself shepherding the company through an IPO or sale. You may be supervising a staff of other attorneys while you help the CEO research new acquisitions and court new investors. Instead of being buried in a conference room stacked with musty legal volumes, you'll be going places and having a blast!

PUBLIC RELATIONS
NO IDEA IS TOO CRAZY!

This might be the right place for you if your job right now is:

- Public/media relations agent
- Account executive
- Account supervisor
- Account manager
- Assistants or junior types
- Vice president of any of the above
- Client services
- Account director
- Staff PR person for some other kind of company

Overview

Public relations is vital to the growth of an up-and-coming Internet company and goes way beyond the traditional practice of sending out boatloads of press releases hoping someone will write a story about your client.

PR on the Internet means high-level strategizing (and, of course, execution) about how a company presents itself directly to the consumers. Besides working the traditional "media relations" angle (what CEO *doesn't* want to be interviewed by Katie Couric?), you've got to create that intangible buzz, using every tool in your toolbox—and making up a bunch of new ones.

Within an Internet firm, public relations usually falls under the advertising/marketing area, but it's rarely a department that's staffed early on (for more on advertising and marketing, flip back to chapter 7). We've heard of companies growing to over four hundred employees before a single PR person is on staff. At some point, these Goliaths may create a position or two, but start-ups (as well as many more-established companies) will rely on crackerjack outside firms to help them with brand building and positioning.

Public relations can cover a vast range of services—and tactics. One start-up company, for example, had its staffers streak through New York's Penn Station during rush hour just to make the six o'clock news! Then there are more traditional attention-getting venues like writing op-ed pieces; getting involved in politics; throwing fund-raisers, parties, and events; and arranging conference appearances and booths. Top PR agencies also assist clients with daily briefings about the industry and their competitors.

So where are the jobs? Some are at traditional PR companies that now handle Internet accounts (if you're already at an agency, this is certainly the easiest move). However, some of these old-guard firms don't treat the Internet like the new phenomenon it is and work it like any traditional client, which is hardly the most effective approach. Try to get a good handle on a firm's Internet philosophy before you sign on.

Some of the most vibrant, creative work is being done by new PR agencies who handle Internet clients exclusively. Currently, there are *so* few of these specialty firms and *so* many potential clients, the agencies can be *very* choosy about who they work with, and they are very expensive! This is a quickly growing field, with (at this writing) virtually all agencies based in either New York or Silicon Valley.

What the Work Is Like

You'll never work in a more fast-paced environment than the world of Internet-oriented public relations. If you don't thrive on urgency, look elsewhere. Stories break twenty-four hours a day, and you'll need to be on top of what's happening at all times, keeping an eye out for the interests of the company or your client. Get used to wearing a pager: You'll have to respond to phone calls and e-mails quickly (whether they come in during business hours or not!), or opportunities will be lost.

To succeed in Internet PR, you need a wide-ranging understanding of the industry, including the technology. A primary part of your job will be to educate journalists, so if you yourself don't get it, you'll have a tough time explaining it to the less enlightened.

Naturally, you've got to be *muy* creative. The PR companies that cut through the clutter score with outlandish stuff that gets them—and their client—noticed. Some of our favorite (and now-legendary) stunts come from Richard Laermer, CEO of RLM Public Relations. They include a billboard on California's Highway 101 asking for funding for a dot-com start-up; the urban delivery service Kozmo.com delivering ice cream in less than an hour to a boardroom full of venture capitalists; launching Nerve.com (a literary sex site) on the same day the Communications Decency Act was struck down by the Supreme Court. Internet PR demands that you reinvent the rules.

You also need a clear understanding of the story angles for different outlets: What appeals to a consumer reporter versus a tech specialist? What makes for a great human-interest story? Cut to the chase quickly, and know whom you're going after.

Because this world moves so fast, you'll need to gather your tools, get the background, then go do your job without elaborate marching orders from someone else. "Be self-sufficient and low maintenance" is Richard's key advice. This doesn't mean acting as a lone wolf: The best public-relations firms thrive on teamwork, sharing contacts, ideas, and information to maximize opportunities for the client. This is a far cry from many of the traditional PR firms, which may have a designated hierarchy of "client contacts." If you have old-world PR experience, you probably spent years stuffing envelopes and answering phones before you got to do the fun stuff. Not so in the Internet world!

Don't Get Hung Up On

MACINTOSH
In fact, if you're Mac-compatible, don't even mention it.

LEARNING ANY SPECIFIC CONTACT-MANAGEMENT SOFTWARE
You'll need to use theirs.

THOSE BIG OLD MEDIA-CONTACT BOOKS
They're dead; you'll be using a digital database.

Typical Compensation

It all depends on where you'll be working. A traditional PR agency with Internet accounts will compensate you as it compensates staff who work with more traditional clients, which is to say a good salary, benefits, and some job security.

At an Internet PR company, however, you may have a unique financial opportunity, because many of the savvier agencies are getting stock options from their *clients* and sharing them with staff. Salaries are competitive with traditional PR companies, and frequently include equity as well. So ask for options and bonuses—there should be plenty for all.

Interview Questions and Concerns to Be Prepared For

- What accounts have you worked on before?

- What level of responsibility did you have?

- What is your proudest PR accomplishment?

- How much time do you spend on the Internet?

- What are your favorite sites?

- What do you know about our company (or agency)?

- (For an agency) Do you know our client list?

- What do you think of our company's or client's positioning?

- What would you do differently?

- How well do you work in a team? Give me an example.

- What do you think of_____trends in the Internet industry? (could be anything!)

- Hypothetical: If you were pitching this kind of client, what ideas might you have?

- How would you do research on the company, the industry?

Get to Know

Go back and re-read every one of our specialty chapters, then review all of the general Internet sites that we recommend in "Resources." As the public-relations professional in the Internet space, you'll be expected to understand all the basics of the business, plus be up on the latest industry trends and buzz. So read and absorb everything you can.

In addition, you should have the following basics under your belt.

GENERAL PRINCIPLES OF PUBLIC RELATIONS

You'll need to know how to tailor your message to a targeted audience, to unearth relevant contacts and get their attention, to make a good impression, to follow up, and to nurture client relationships.

BE AN EXCELLENT WRITER AND COMMUNICATOR

Whether it's a written communication or a verbal one, get your points across clearly and quickly. There's no time to learn this on the job; you've got to bring this to the table.

RULES OF NETIQUETTE

Never send an attachment to someone who doesn't know you, and virus scan your computer daily so you don't unwittingly send a computer bug to anyone. These are just two of the rules as they apply to public relations; there are numerous Web sites that can teach you more of the basics. Plus, every firm will have its own way of doing things.

Where Can You Go from Here?

Public relations is one of the fastest-growing subspecialties in the Internet. If you do great things at a PR agency, you can go start your own firm or run the PR department for an Internet company. If you demonstrate your ability to contribute beyond the traditional realm of public relations, you can easily rise to higher levels of responsibility in advertising and marketing—and you'll never have so much fun!

THE COMMUNITY ORGANIZER
EVERYBODY GET TOGETHER . . . RIGHT NOW

This might be the right place for you if your job right now is:

Your prior career experience isn't as big a deal here. A former cop with a passionate interest in growing tulips can be a terrific organizer of a gardening community. Instead, these are the preferred *qualities* for a community organizer.

- Must like people

- Likes being on the Internet at home (it can involve some wacky hours); also helps to have a speedy and reliable Internet connection

- Has a special interest in and knowledge of the topic

- Self-starter

Overview

The community organizer is something of a brand-new Internet species, and people with all kinds of backgrounds—from teachers and reporters to stay-at-home moms—are succeeding in this area.

What do they do? Very simply, they "organize" and oversee an online area that deals with a particular interest or specialty. The Web is built on the idea of "community," where people sharing a common interest get together no matter where they live and swap information, photos, files, favorite links about that subject, and more. The community organizer's job is to make that virtual gathering a great experience. This can involve researching and locating other links, moderating chat sessions or bulletin boards, providing advice and feedback to the respondents, and creating or digging up appropriate content for that area. They bring inspiration to the site; they're cheerleaders, keeping the dialogue going and making everyone feel welcome.

Here's just a small sampling of the special-interest areas out there a community organizer might focus on:

- Specific diseases, ailments, and syndromes
- Professional sports of every sort, including local teams and individual athletes
- Leisure-time activities, like fishing and knitting
- Collectors of almost anything
- Music, and all its varieties (heavy metal to Mozart)
- Ethnic groups, including expatriates
- Professional and career groups

- Every stage of parenting, from thinking about it through coping with adult children

- Support groups for addictions

- Diet and fitness programs and support groups

- Caring for sick or elderly people

- Disabled people

- Kids and teenagers

- Religious groups

- Political interest

- Financial and stock-tip groups

- Travelers

- Mental help and therapy communities

As the Internet began to grow, plenty of early adopter volunteers were ready, willing, and able to take on the role of community guru for free. It was fun, you were "cool," and your Internet service was usually on the house. AOL, for example, still uses volunteers, as do other community sites—such as iVillage, the Women's Network.

As the Web matures, the responsibilities of running a truly top-notch community at a heavily trafficked site are too complex and involved for part-time volunteers alone. Organizers do everything from arranging and monitoring chats and keeping up with activity on message boards to writing newsletters. Finally, and most importantly, they're paid for the work.

Every site with paid community positions handles it differently. In some organizations, it's considered "editorial" work. In others, there may be a special division called "community." Job titles and responsibilities vary widely. Some sites expect you to do all the work from home, a few want to see your face in the office. Most all offer training and support.

What the Work Is Like (for Most!)

Most community organizers begin as volunteers. They're interested in the subject, get involved, and spend a lot of time at a particular site. It's rare that a David start-up is in a position to pay these early activists, even though it's largely *their* dedication that helps the site flourish. You'll have better luck at a Goliath.

If you *do* move from volunteer status to paid professional, you'll likely work from home, monitoring and directing the activity within this community. You'll set up the chats and then run them, making sure the participants stay on topic and follow the rules. You'll be in charge of message boards, making sure that flames or spam are removed and company policies are enforced. You may need to write content, like a daily blurb about what's happening or perhaps a weekly newsletter for the community.

You'll be responsible for recruiting volunteers to help you. On some active sites, one person is responsible for monitoring up to forty different message boards, so he or she will need trusted volunteers to help manage day to day details.

The community organizer is the liaison between the company and the participants in his or her community. You'll be the one to police things and make sure everyone is playing nicely. You'll introduce new tools or different parts of the site that you think might enrich user experience. But you're also the conduit from community members back to the company: Are they complaining that the site is sending them too many e-mails every month? You'll need to relate that back to management.

As the resident expert, it's critical you keep up with what's going on. You may recruit experts to come in for scheduled chats or to write a guest column. If your group consists of parents of toddlers, for example, you'll need to be familiar with *all* points of view on potty training—and make sure that voices from all sides get the floor (yes, people get very indignant when they can't express their ideas on this subject!).

"Community" is the very definition of stickiness on a Web site—a place people visit frequently and a place where they linger. This makes it extremely valuable to advertisers and investors. A big part of your job is to make people feel that they belong and have a relationship with you and the others in the community. It's an important job, but the best part is, if you like your topic, it doesn't feel like work!

Don't Get Hung Up On

You don't need to know HTML or anything fancy. There will be Web-based forms to make it easy for you to do any administration of the Web site.

Typical Compensation

The good news is that most community organizers love their work. The bad news is that most are vastly underpaid, considering the number of hours they put in.

Unfortunately, pay for this position is so variable that we can't offer a specific outline for how the jobs and pay are structured. You may be paid based on traffic or revenue to your area. If you work from home, expect to be paid as if it were a part-time job, even if you spend a minimum of forty hours on the job every week. That time will be flexible, of course: You can usually do it between carpool runs and loads of laundry—just as long as you get the job done.

The company should supply you with a good computer and a fast Internet connection. You should also be eligible for stock options and bonuses, as well as a benefits package—if there is one.

Interview Questions and Concerns to Be Prepared For

Here's a cool thing about interviewing for a community organizer job: It's likely to be conducted entirely by e-mail, with possibly a phone call or two and only occasionally a face-to-face meeting. Consider it a dress rehearsal, with your virtual communications skills on display, and be ready for questions like:

- How long have you been a member of our site?

- How long have you been participating in our community?

- What activities have you done in our community?

- Do you visit other communities? Which ones?

- Are any of them doing things that we ought to be doing?

- Why do you want to be a community organizer?

- Do you like people?

- How do you handle grouchy, complaining people?

- Are you a good speller?

- Do you write well?

- How many hours can you commit to working with us?

- Can you come to a conference once a year (or more)?

Deep Background

If you want to give this area a try, you're in luck, because there isn't a lot of new stuff you need to learn, other than being up on your topic. Brush up on your basic Web skills and be very proficient with the following:

Chat. Learn chat vocabulary, get comfortable in chat rooms, know the rules of chat on various sites, the difference between public and private chat, chat rooms with guests and open chat, scheduled chat, etc.

E-mail. Learn your e-mail program cold, including how to sort messages into folders, attach documents, download attachments from others, and access your e-mail account from other computers.

File and program downloading. Know how to download a plug-in off the Internet, upgrade your browser, and save and reformat files that have been sent to you.

Instant messaging programs. Try a few of them, find one you like, and get your friends and family on it. Get a feel for what instantaneous interaction is all about, because you'll likely have an instant messaging program open at all times when you're on the job.

Message boards. Visit lots of different boards; see how people are using them. Read the posts; learn the rules.

Personal home pages. Build one or more personal home pages to learn how the systems work. You'll need to provide answers for your community members when they have questions.

Web-based forms. Much of your work will entail filling out forms or following instructions and links from a Web site, so get comfortable with the whole process.

Web-based calendaring programs. Visit a few of these sites and try inputting things like your spouse's birthday or next week's tee-off time. It's likely you'll have to use one of these to interact with your employer and manage your community's activities.

Naturally, we suggest getting familiar with the general sites listed in "Resources," as well as going back and re-reading chapter 6 on creative job opportunities.

Where Can You Go from Here?

Community is growing rapidly within the Internet, so even if the first position you get isn't as lofty as you'd like, hang in there. If you're good and stay committed to the Web site, you can go far. One gal we know went through at least six different positions with the same employer before landing an editorial job at the same Web site. She steadily progressed upward as she proved herself, working from home the whole time.

If your career still doesn't have the kind of upward mobility you were hoping for, remember that good community types are constantly being poached by other Web sites, especially for customer service. This is a fast-track—if sometimes circuitous—path for you if you're committed to this option.

Chapter 10

MISCELLANEOUS NET GIGS
Kitchen Sink 2.0

Let us guess—you've been wildly thumbing through this book looking for your *exact* job match (beekeeper) and have yet to find it. Don't give up and toss the book across the room just yet—Internet careers are only as limited as your thinking.

We've already covered the biggies, the hiring categories that embrace the most typical career paths. However, there are an endless number of subspecialties, too many to name here. Think creatively about the field you work in: There's hardly a business that *isn't* being affected by the dynamic intervention of the Internet. Think about what it is you do, and how it can be transacted in some other way. Someone who fixes cars or cuts hair won't be supplanted by virtual equivalents on the Internet; however, a travel agent or manufacturer's rep will soon find that technology *can* replace them. It's important that you take some time to think through the elements of your current career—whatever it is, from our beekeeper friends to health professionals to artists and beyond—and figure out the Internet angle on it, combining some or all of the elements we've been discussing throughout this book. Just about anyone can take their specialty and make a home for it online.

There's no way we can cover every single Internet job possibility in one book—but here's a rundown of some additional categories and how the Internet is having an effect on them. At the end of each section, we give you some homework and brainstorming ideas; we also suggest spending time at the various sites, reading publications and learning to use the tools listed in "Resources" (p. 259). You take it from there!

☞ WARNING SIGNS THAT THE WEB WILL THREATEN YOUR INDUSTRY[a]

Are you in a highly regulated market? Regulated industries aren't used to competition, which makes them targets for unregulated competitors who can turn legal barriers to entry into legal barriers to compete. Look what happened to the phone company.

Are you in a fragmented market? If you're in a market with many buyers but no dominant sellers and lots of inefficiency, your business is ripe for Internet transformation. Ford, GM, and Daimler Chrysler are now using the Web to buy raw materials for cars—a move that shook up the parts-supplier industry.

Is the product you deal with information-based? The entertainment and financial industries are especially vulnerable because their product never takes physical form.

Are customers in your industry poorly organized? Customers can organize themselves via the Internet and cut out the middleman (you). The auto, real estate, and insurance markets are business arenas in which power currently resides in a complex web of distributors, agents, and brokers. But that may not last forever as customers learn how to buy direct.

[a]Larry Downes, "Intellectual Capital," *The Industry Standard*, March 20, 2000, p. 210.

The Arts

The Internet has been a boon for all areas of the arts, from opera companies to performance artists and independent musicians, from edgy downtown art galleries to auction houses that handle fine antiques.

Live dance performances won't be replaced by an Internet substitute; but with Web access, you can find out performance dates, buy tickets online, read the performers' bios, view streaming videos of a performance, and go into a chat room to discuss what you saw. You can even buy a souvenir program or T-shirt. So although the actual performance (or museum exhibition or live concert) is still a critical part of the experience, the Internet has made the whole thing richer and more meaningful.

MP3 technology is enabling unsigned rock bands to post their albums and develop a bigger following than they'd get playing at local clubs. They can either sell albums directly to fans over the Web or attract a record label who'll sign them and turn them into the next Led Zeppelin (or Carpenters—your choice).

Upscale auction houses use the Internet to share photos of their treasures and reach bidders and dealers beyond those who can attend an auction in person. Never mind all of the stuff auctioned every day on eBay that never would have made it out of the garage!

Arts organizations use the Web to promote events, help in their never-ending fund-raising efforts, and educate the public. The arts scene has a lively new component online.

DO YOUR HOMEWORK

Find out more by using search engines to find Web sites of your favorite arts organizations, bands, artists, and venues. Most localities have Web sites that act as directories for all arts organizations within their community.

THEN DO SOME BRAINSTORMING

- Are there groups or associations of people in your field? Do they have a Web site?

- Does your existing employer have a Web site? Can you work there?

- If you're not the performer but work in a support role in an organization, is there a parallel in the online world?

- What bigger portal or general-interest sites have sections devoted to your area?

- What kind of Web site would benefit from your knowledge and contacts?

Health and Fitness

The last decade or so has seen an explosion in healthier living as people take more interest and responsibility for their own wellness. Whether it's a reaction to skyrocketing health-care costs or just the baby boomers' recognizing their own mortality, the Internet as a resource couldn't have come at a better time.

There are literally thousands of sites providing all kinds of information on everything from serious illnesses to the best exercises for flattening your tummy. One of the big controversies in this arena is the reliability of online health information. What's the source: responsible medical professionals, a pharmaceutical company, or just a flaky healer from who-knows-where?

E-commerce has really exploded within the health category:

You can buy vitamins and herbal supplements online—and research what each will do for your body. Want to learn more about Reiki or other alternative practices? Not only can you find plenty of information on esoteric treatments but you can also locate a practitioner. Fitness-oriented sites have tools to calculate your body fat and ideal weight (don't go there right after Thanksgiving!), design a healthy diet, and e-mail you a daily or weekly dose of encouragement. You can get tips from the pros on exercise, the best ways to quit smoking, or what to expect at each stage of pregnancy. And you'll probably find a community of people who've either been there, done that, or are experiencing it now and can offer some moral support, along with information.

There are hundreds of sites devoted to specific medical conditions, like breast cancer, AIDS, and chronic fatigue. You'll find the latest medical information, frequently from accredited organizations (again, check the source). You'll also find chat and bulletin board features that create a support community—especially valuable for people unable to leave their homes. One of Cindy's friends, diagnosed with Lou Gehrig's disease, found that the Internet became a precious lifeline, especially when the disease progressed to the point where he was unable to get around. Not only did he have access to vital information about his condition but he had others who had been through the very same thing to support him during the rough patches (and on the Internet, there's always someone awake and ready to chat).

As we empower ourselves and become more active partners in our health, the Web provides the kinds of information once only accessible to medical professionals: You can find out drug side-effects and decode medical jargon. Some sites will e-mail you reminders to make appointments or take medication and allow doctors instant emergency access to your medical history. Your insurance company probably has a Web site where you can research your doctor's credentials and find specialists who participate in the plan.

Physicians are making themselves more accessible by participating in live online chats or by sending newsletters on their latest findings and advice. The Internet has become a powerful tool for them to offer more attention to patients than they could offer during an office visit—and for ensuring that those patients have the information to make more informed choices.

DO YOUR HOMEWORK

There are so many health and fitness sites out there, we won't even attempt to name names. It's not hard to find them, but check carefully to see who's behind the site and what their motivation is before you believe everything they say.

THEN DO SOME BRAINSTORMING

- Which Web sites seem most in keeping with your interests and point of view?

- What could you bring to them?

- What bigger general-interest sites could benefit from your expertise and knowledge?

- As a health-care professional, could you consult with patients over the Internet? Or use the Internet to reach new patients?

- Could you support a community? (See chapter 9.)

Finance

The Internet is revolutionizing everything about the way Wall Street does business. The average consumer is suddenly empowered to buy, sell, and trade securities; do the research; and execute transactions,—all without the traditional broker.

Charles Schwab was among the first to let its clients get in on the act, providing access to current market information and enabling online trading. Now every old-line brokerage and a whole host of new online-only brokerages have sprung up, with varying degrees of research and content, and different pricing strategies. It's an out-and-out war.

Information flows as fast as a stock ticker: You can get the latest numbers on a mutual fund, access electronic versions of financial magazines and newspapers, or participate in live chats with the hot investment adviser of the week. You won't find any shortage of Web sites serving the do-it-yourself online investor.

Your mutual fund company probably has your fund records online to let you transfer money electronically into the account, so you can add to your retirement plan without ever leaving your desk.

Is real estate your area? Buyers and sellers can now conduct business over the Internet without ever leaving home. Shop for the best mortgage rates, locate a realtor, and take a virtual tour of a property. The same goes for other big-ticket items like cars: You can hear what the safety experts say about your dream wheels, finance it, find the best insurance rates, make a bid, and literally have the car delivered to your house.

Banks are feeling the impact of the Internet, too. How about online bill paying to save you the hassle of writing checks and looking for a stamp twice a month? Brick-and-mortar banks are moving in this direction, and now there are virtual banking institutions like wingspan.com and telebank.com.

Insurance companies are scrambling, too (see "Warning Signs" on p. 168). Consumers used to be captive to their friendly neighborhood insurance agent. Now they can comparison-shop online, entering their particulars to get information and price quotes.

The bottom line on the bottom line is this: The Internet has become a key tool in achieving the American Dream. By providing easy, thorough access to useful resources and information, consumers become better informed, more confident—and more likely to buy or invest.

DO YOUR HOMEWORK

Whatever your specific area—investing, banking, insurance, mutual funds—there are dozens of sites to investigate to learn about the latest trends and competitive factors.

THEN DO SOME BRAINSTORMING

- Does your current employer have an Internet division? Is it making smart moves? Could you bring what you do to its Internet site?

- Are your financial-industry skills transferable to Internet companies that do other things? Go back and read our various specialty chapters: Deal makers might like business development; a business analyst might do well in e-commerce or operations. Get creative!

Travel/Hospitality

Remember planning a trip in the old days? You'd call up your travel agent who'd research destinations for you, maybe send you some brochures in the mail. You'd decide where you wanted to go, and put yourself in the agent's hands, hoping he or she booked what you had in mind at the best rate possible.

Now every wired consumer has access to the same information

as that travel agent (an increasingly obsolete job description). The Internet offers better, more complete, and more timely information than the stuff your travel agent had. Various sites let you track your frequent-flier miles, find an online currency converter, get the latest weather reports, even transmit the departure status of an upcoming flight to a pager. There are sites that help business travelers plan meetings in other cities by recommending potential locations and available dates, then let you book it over the Internet. The site even e-mails all invitees with the details. It's no wonder that do-it-yourself Internet travel planning has increased a whopping 1,500 percent in just about four years![1]

Before you visit a new city, find the cool places to go, maybe even see a streaming video clip of the new baby animals born last week at the San Diego Zoo or the running of the bulls in Pamplona.

To help you get around, download and print out a map or driving directions. Of course, you'll be hungry after the zoo, so click to reserve a table at the hottest restaurant in town—after reading an online review, of course. And when you get back to your hotel, the in-room massage you booked via e-mail will be waiting for you.

The Internet is making travel ever more convenient and exciting for consumers. About the only thing it *can't* do for you (so far) is make sure your luggage doesn't get lost.

DO YOUR HOMEWORK

Every airline, hotel chain, and car rental company has a major Web presence. Check out the general-interest travel sites associated with the print magazines and the new online-only travel

---

1. "Travelers Use Internet to Plan Trips," *BizReport.com.* February 9, 2000.

destinations. Look at the Internet guides to specific areas—and don't forget to check out online mapping!

THEN DO SOME BRAINSTORMING

First, if you're a travel agent, read this book from cover to cover. The Internet is changing the way your industry works, but because you're probably already computer savvy, it shouldn't be hard to make the leap into something with a real future.

Working in the hospitality industry (including restaurants) basically demands that you be nice to surly people on a daily basis—which is just what the customer-service area of the Internet needs. There's a huge demand for your good humor, so go back and read chapter 8 on e-commerce.

Is the city or company you work for on the Web yet? Help them get hooked up, then help them market their Web site to the major travel portals.

Education

As of 1998, the Department of Education estimated that 51 percent of American classrooms had Internet connections.[2] That number is growing every month as more and more educators adopt the Internet as a vital learning and communication tool.

Although bigger school districts have extensive technology departments and specialized training on using the Internet as a teaching tool, in rural areas or under-funded inner cities, teachers are forced to learn on the fly. But there's no doubt that kids love computers, and the resources of the Internet open up worlds beyond the classroom. A fourth grader doing a report on Alaska can learn about dog sleds, weather patterns, and glaciers, then find an

---

2. Big Surf in a Little School, *Newsweek*, September 20, 1999, p. 64.

online buddy from a school in Anchorage. Content sites have sprung up specifically to help kids with their homework (no, we're not talking about selling term papers).

Schools are using the Internet as a communication tool by posting the school calendar online or creating e-mail lists for snow days. Teachers are using it to connect with each other, too: Now they can find another English teacher trying to make *The Scarlet Letter* work in a high school classroom!

No college can get away without a Web site to attract prospective students. More and more are even accepting applications online (although they print them out later).

Distance learning is the ability to take courses in almost any subject without physically being in the same location as the instructor or other students. There's plenty of debate on whether this is a good thing, but when institutions like Columbia University begin to license their courses for use on the Internet, it becomes a trend that must be taken seriously.

As more classrooms get wired, the Internet will offer opportunities for even cooler stuff. Stay tuned!

DO YOUR HOMEWORK

Check out some school Web sites. What are they trying to do? What about sites geared to students? Do they get it right? Investigate some of the courses offered online—then take one!

THEN DO SOME BRAINSTORMING

- Your school district may just be waiting for a champion to make this Internet thing happen—could that be you?

- Could you teach over the Internet?

- Does your knowledge of a specific topic make you a natural expert for a content Web site (e.g., a science teacher working for space.com)?

- What else about your experience in education is transferable?

Politics and Government

The Internet became a force to be reckoned with in the U.S. political arena in 1998 when Jesse "The Body" Ventura got himself elected governor of Minnesota. An independent candidate with no traditional organization to back him up, Ventura had a primitive Web site and an enormously efficient e-mail list that fueled interest in him and collected thousands of contributions. This unlikely success was a wake-up call to politicos across the country, and soon every contender for the 2000 presidential race had a Web strategy to keep him in front of the digital contingent. You'd be hardpressed to find a candidate for any election at a state level or higher who *doesn't* have a campaign Web site.

The news organizations and different interest groups also have sites that offer information, candidate matching, chats, and discussion boards so visitors can conduct heated political debates across virtual dining-room tables. Candidates make hosted chat appearances on important sites. The Internet is the minute-to-minute information sources for political junkies.

Once elected, politicians find the Internet a very useful tool for staying in touch with constituents. They offer FAQs for things that people ask every day (saving their staff hundreds of annoying phone calls) and links to government sites that can answer other specific questions.

And at every level of government, bureaucrats are trying to figure out how to use the Internet to do business. One early fiasco was when the Social Security Administration put everyone's accounts online—without any security. If you knew your brother-in-law's social security number, you could check his earnings history. (Don't worry—it came down after a few days!)

That gaffe notwithstanding, the government is working on some really good uses of the Internet. Arizona lets you re-register your motor vehicle via the Web, for example. What we wouldn't give to never stand in a motor vehicles line again! How about virtual voting? It's all coming, and you can find plenty of other interesting experiments out there already. Some day our kids will read this section and laugh loudly that anyone thought this was cutting edge.

DO YOUR HOMEWORK

Visit the top candidates' Web sites and read up on their strategies. Check out your local representatives and see what they're up to. Then look into the federal, state, and local governments and find out what services they're offering (or not!).

THEN DO SOME BRAINSTORMING

- What do you know how to do? Is anyone doing it on the Web?

- Can you help bring your government agency or candidate onto the Web?

- Will your insider knowledge of how it all works be valuable to a certain kind of site?

- And again, if you're used to doing customer service, there's lots of opportunity for a job switch into e-commerce! (See chapter 8.)

Did We Neglect Your Occupational Area?

If you think of things we haven't thought of yet, please e-mail us at authors@notjustgeeks.com and we'll include it in our next edition!

Chapter 11

WORKING ON THE WEB—WITHOUT GIVING UP YOUR PARKING SPACE

When You're Not Ready to Go All the Way

The Internet business excites you. You want in. Only problem is you're not a big risk taker or you've got financial commitments that don't let you roll those virtual dice and risk missing a paycheck or two.

Well, there's another option: working for a traditional business in its Web department—perhaps the company that employs you right now. In fact, we think this approach works best with your present employer so you won't have to master Internet skills *and* learn a whole new company's business at the same time.

Depending on where you live, you may find that the only Internet-related jobs may be at one of these not-coms. Currently, there just aren't that many start-up Internet firms outside of New York, California, and a few other major cities. We'll talk in more detail about where the jobs are in the next chapter.

While you'll rarely see the (potentially) big payoffs in stock options you'd get at a pure dot-com, working the Web at a brick-and-mortar firm offers the chance to try something cutting edge, get some hands-on Internet experience, and keep your benefits (along with that reserved parking space). And if you *really* make something happen while you're there, you'll be sitting pretty: You will either have turbo-charged your career in that same firm or be very well positioned to pitch a job at almost any Internet company.

If you haven't done so already, read our take on the specific Internet hiring areas (chapters 3 through 10). That information will *usually* apply to the Internet department of a traditional company, too. However, there are some key differences between an Internet career at a dot-com and one within a not-com.

Overview

It's pretty hard to find any company that hasn't tried to get its arms around this Internet thing—even if it doesn't actually do very much with it. If you're considering a Web-oriented position at your firm, you'll want to know what its approach is to the Internet. Some key questions to ask include the following:

WILL THIS BE PART OF THE MAIN COMPANY OR A SEPARATE DIVISION?

How does your company treat the Internet group? Is it a department within the existing corporate structure or its own freestanding company?

For retailers, that might mean a department devoted to the Internet as a sales channel or it could mean a whole new division set up to *compete* with traditional sales channels. For example, Barnes and Noble and bn.com are entirely different companies, but nordstrom.com is part of the Nordstrom department stores: You can return shoes ordered on their Internet site to their store in the mall. How does this issue of "multiple channels" play out where you'll be working?

If you remain part of the main company, there will be other integration issues, such as how your financial reporting interfaces with the rest of the firm, and how your merchandise and inventory are handled. You won't be making decisions in a vacuum, because what you do will certainly have an effect and be affected by other concerns critical to the larger company's bottom line. According to our sources, it's ideal if the Internet department has an oversight or steering committee made up of members from other departments: It's a sign that the Web presence is being supported and fully integrated into the company.

The extent of the involvement that other departments will exercise is also something you need to know. Will the communications group be supplying Web copy? Who's responsible for staffing the positions? Understand how different departments will be interacting with the Web group.

WHAT'S THE COMPANY TRYING TO ACCOMPLISH ON THE WEB?

Lots of companies are using the Internet either as a new way to peddle their wares or to lower the cost of doing business. For instance, UPS offers online package tracking, which shifts an enormous customer-service burden back to consumers and saves UPS millions of dollars.

Some companies merely use the Internet as a basic publicity or marketing tool and don't expect much return on investment. (Our advice: Stay away from these companies; they don't understand the full power of the medium and you won't learn enough there to make it worth your while.) Spend some time searching your company's PR materials to see what it's saying publicly about the Web and how it plans to use it.

☞ HOW THE INTERNET WILL AFFECT A NOT-COM (MAYBE YOURS?)

In the February 14, 2000, issue of *Business Week,* an article titled "Why the Productivity Revolution Will Spread" outlined some key ways traditional businesses are using the new technology (maybe you can steal one of these ideas for your company!).[a]

Innovation. Generate new business ideas and improvements by collecting suggestions from employees via e-mail. Royal Dutch/Shell's companywide contest resulted in a new method for finding oil.

Collaboration. An extranet can more efficiently relay critical information between a company and its outside partners. The results of this innovation for Ocean Spray include cutting waste and boosting productivity among its growers, who now reap higher profits.

Design. Web technology allows for faster design of prototypes. Honeywell is one company using this, cutting its previous design time from six months to twenty-four hours.

Purchasing. Ford Motor Company has replaced its complex purchasing network of personal contacts and complicated forms with a global electronic forum where deals can be made instantly. The savings amount to billions.

Logistics. Cement maker Cemex uses a Web-based truck-dispatch system to reduce delivery time from three hours to twenty minutes.

Marketing. The data-mining abilities of the Internet are perfect for finely targeting marketing efforts and customer service. A Wisconsin door factory uses the Web to focus on only its very best clients. It cut its customer roster in half—but doubled order volumes.

Service. Customers can communicate their exact specifications and needs to the company via the Internet. GE Power Systems, for example, holds virtual meetings with its customers, who can see blueprints, order changes, and follow the actual manufacturing process of turbine engines.

[a]Jennifer Reingold and Marcia Stepanek with Diane Brady, "Why the Productivity Revolution Will Spread," *Business Week*, February 14, 2000, p. 116.

HOW IMPORTANT TO THE PARENT COMPANY IS THIS VENTURE AND HOW WELL IS IT FUNDED?

Some traditional companies still treat the Internet like a passing fad: They put the boss's nephew in charge and allocate as few dollars for it as possible. Obviously, you won't get very far in a situation like that. And it's a bad sign if the rest of the company doesn't have Internet access at their desks—that's a sure sign that top management doesn't see it as important to the company.

A good Web site and the marketing, promotion, and partnerships required to make it soar demand at least a medium-term investment at the highest level of the company. Ideally, you'd like to know that the Internet effort has been cleared as a budget line— even better, that there are few, if any, budget constraints. Although it's always preferable for the Web division to exist in a different location (more freedom), you'd like to know that it reports to the top and isn't out of sight, out of mind.

HOW INDEPENDENT IS THE INTERNET GROUP?

Enlightened companies fund their Internet groups generously and allow them to become a hothouse of new ideas. Less visionary companies create a bare-bones group and look for a quick payoff. Know the expectations.

What the Work Is Like

CORPORATE CULTURE

When you work for a dot-com, you expect pandemonium. Whether a firm is a David in full start-up mode or a Goliath growing faster than anyone anticipated, the workplace is usually loose, the structure and responsibilities ever changing.

It ain't necessarily so for the Internet department of an established firm: A budget has been set for the group and each position accounted for with a nice, clean org chart. Not that every firm will stick to it, but assume that your job will be fairly structured. At times, you may have to take on extra work, particularly at year end, until the new fiscal year allows for new hires. This rarely happens at start-ups, which just hire bodies when they need them and have the money to do so.

Or you might find something completely different: Victor was hired by a major phone company to help develop its new Web initiative. Five positions had been authorized for the department, and his was one of them. While the honchos had lots of enthusiasm, no one had strategized beyond "get us on the Internet!" He had no mandate, no real assignment. Victor sat in his brand-new window office for a month, throwing pencils at the ceiling tiles; then he got himself transferred into a new position where there was actually something to accomplish.

The corporate culture within a firm's Internet group usually won't be as loosey-goosey as their brethren at a dot-com; where, for example, they dress casually; your attire will more closely mimic the rest of the company. Don't look for things like Foosball tables or beer nights, either, although some of the smarter brick-and-mortars give their Internet departments enough autonomy to feel hipper than the parent firm.

Nigel was invited to lots and lots of meetings at *his* not-com. Big Brother's culture required every meeting organizer to invite everyone they could possibly think of who might somehow be affected. It was an enormous waste of Nigel's time, so when he got an invitation, he started asking why. If there was a valid reason for his presence, he'd go. If not, he'd blow it off and focus on what was important to his job. Now everyone in the Internet group does it, and they're much more efficient as a result.

The Internet group will likely attract others from within the company, and that inevitably means office politics, history, and baggage—things that are not so much a part of a pure play. Decisions may take longer as they go through multiple layers of approval—another thing you don't find much of at a dot-com, at least a David (Goliaths can get as bogged down in bureaucracy as anyone!).

The upside to this is that these people will already know how to get things done. The fact that your company already has a reputation in the marketplace should make it easier for the Internet effort to become successful. After all, no one's developing relationships from scratch.

PAY AND BENEFITS

Not-coms that are serious about becoming Internet players understand they need talent—and that they have to pay for it to complete with mass defections to the dot-coms. Because they generally don't have pre-IPO equity to parcel out, they may well offer higher salaries and better bonus packages. If the compensation package doesn't seem competitive, ask why. It should be; you can find one if you look.

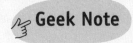 **Geek Note** Many not-coms have begun issuing tracking stocks, which allow them to chart the performance of their Internet divisions separately from their core businesses. The idea is to unlock the value of their Internet businesses for shareholders. Sprint did this; so has the *New York Times*, which hoped to raise $100 million by issuing a tracking stock for Times Company Digital.[a] So there may actually be some equity opportunity at not-coms if you can get a share of this action.

[a]"Closing Bell," *Business Week*, February 14, 2000, p. 54.

At a dot-com, individual bonuses tied to company performance can be "iffy"—who knows if a given start-up is going to fly? Tying them to the solid revenue performance of a brick and mortar can work to your advantage. Just remember that your company may already have a predetermined top limit.

Working in the Internet division at a not-com, you'll enjoy all the fun of working on the cutting edge, plus the comforting perks of a traditional company: Regular paychecks, corporate benefits, an office, a computer, and MIS staff to help you out in a pinch. If you travel, there'll be a corporate travel agent and an account with a car service, a car rental company, the works. Do *not* pooh-pooh the importance of these: Once you've spent an entire afternoon searching online for the cheapest fare for a business trip, you'll fully appreciate the value of having your ticket paid by corporate credit card and delivered by messenger—with just a phone call.

Now if after all this, you still feel that going for an Internet position within your current firm is not "really" joining the dot-com party, consider this: Many *Fortune* 500 companies are rapidly gaining ground on their dot-com-petition. A lot of experts feel that corporations have the money, infrastructure, and brand names to win the Internet race over the long haul.[1] The stock-market stakeout of dot-coms certainly should give you pause. So take another look around your office; it may very well be the smartest place to take those first steps onto the Internet.

---

1. Mel Duvall, "Will Dot Coms Face Revenge of the Dinosaurs?" *Interactive Week*, September 6, 1999, p. 14.

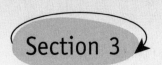
Section 3

GET READY, GET SET . . .

The resources available on the Internet have added incredible depth to today's job-seeking process. No more long hours at the library digging through moldy back issues of trade journals— these days you can log on and find the most current press releases, financial reports, and news about the company players. And you *must* be current if you're going to pitch an Internet job.

It's all really helpful, but such an embarrassment of riches can also leave you feeling as overwhelmed as a week at Mardi Gras. In this section, we'll help you cut through the clutter to quickly locate the information you need to land the perfect Internet job. You'll learn the best ways to get to the right people at the right companies, and how to present yourself when you do.

Among the things we'll cover:

- Do you really need your own Web page?

- What skills and accomplishments should you highlight on your résumé to make 'em want you—even if you have no Internet experience?

- Should you use an Internet headhunter? How do you find the right one?

- What's the best way to use e-mail to land a job . . . and what will instantly kill your prospects?

- Do those job sites really work?

- How can you locate the companies that best match who you are and what you want?

- What trade publications and organizations do you need to know?

- How to get to the person with the authority to hire you. (Hint: She's not in human resources.)

By the end of this section, you'll be loaded for bear and that much closer to your dream job!

Chapter 12

THE RECONNAISSANCE MISSION
Panning for Information Gold

When we told people what our book was about, we got some blank stares. After all, isn't hunting down an Internet job just like looking for any other kind of work? Obviously we feel the answer is a resounding "no."

Certainly some rules always apply, whether you're looking in the traditional or the digital world. You need to exercise common courtesy, do your homework ahead of time, and have a strong résumé. However, the Internet offers far more resources for conducting a fruitful job search. Besides headhunters, there are news groups, job boards, and e-mail lists to take advantage of. You may not be able to get a bigwig on the phone, but you just might capture their attention with an effectively worded e-mail—and get the interview. We'll cover an arsenal of job-search skills later in the chapter, but before you can make the best use of it, let's hone your focus.

What Kind of Company Are You Best Suited For?

Your response may be "Any one with a generous employee stock option plan," but money isn't everything. If you're a sales whiz, you won't be happy at a site specializing in online book reviews. Conversely, writerly types won't exactly thrive at a site that sells computer software. Look over the business models that we covered back in chapter 1 and think hard about the kind of environment you'd do best in. Also, do some brainstorming outside the box: What are your favorite sites? What companies have you heard about recently that sound interesting? Maybe your opportunity lies there; use the resources we describe later on to begin networking and make a contact.

ARE YOU A DAVID OR GOLIATH?

Part of knowing what kind of company you'd thrive at is knowing your tolerance for risk. Are you prepared to deal with a sudden change in your job status, or do you have obligations (a family, kids in college) that would make that too stressful? Can you keep a lot of balls in the air, or do you prefer focusing on one thing at a time? Be honest with yourself and assess whether you really *would* thrive in the chaotic, unpredictable world of the David companies—or if the (somewhat) more stable Goliath firm is a better fit.

WHAT GETS YOU BUZZED?

What are you passionate about? The Internet is an entrepreneurial environment, and employers are looking for people who are excited about the work they do. Yes, everyone is interested in making money—but creativity and freedom really drive the biggest part of the Internet world. "Passion" also goes a long way in getting you through some of the challenges of the Internet work environment, such as long hours, less-than-ideal offices, and sudden change.

Identify Companies You'd Like to Work For

Your first question is probably, "Where are the jobs?" In the United States, most dot-com jobs are clustered on the coasts. California's Silicon Valley is the original hotbed of high-tech development, but New York's Silicon Alley isn't far behind. And with Microsoft leading the way, Seattle is home to a lot of activity as well.

There are lively Internet scenes in these other U.S. areas as well:

- Boston and the Route 128 corridor
- Los Angeles
- Dallas
- Chicago
- Atlanta
- Denver
- Salt Lake City
- New York suburbs, including New Jersey, Connecticut, and Long Island
- Baltimore/Washington/Northern Virginia
- Research Triangle, North Carolina
- Austin

If you live somewhere else, there are still plenty of opportunities—you just have to look harder for them (and, conversely, they have to look a lot harder for candidates, which gives you a leg up!). Internet employment outside these regions is more likely to be at a not-com, but that's still a respectable way to get your start.

How do you find Internet jobs in a particular area? All job-listing sites allow you to sort opportunities by geography. Yahoo also has a feature called "Get Local," with links to resources in a specified locality. Use this as your starting point and start exploring. Or check your local newspaper's site, which often has directories and guides to who's doing what on the Internet. Seek out cybercafés, networks, and organizations. Go to their meetings, introduce yourself, and ask them about companies near you that are doing interesting things. In more active locales, you're likely to find formal or informal networks of Internet workers, a great resource for information on what companies are out there or are just starting up. If you hear about an interesting company, but can't find out where it's located (some company Web sites won't tell you), go to http://www.networksolutions.com for information on where the domain name is registered.

Okay, we hesitate to even put this one in, but you *can* find Internet jobs in the old-fashioned printed newspaper classifieds (which are almost always online, too). Many of these may be low-level, entry positions, but we *do* know of one guy who found his dream job in Grand Rapids by reading the Sunday paper. You just never know.

Use your ingenuity. No matter how remote your town is, there's a local telephone company, a local cable company, an online newspaper, or an ISP, and they all need staff. Investigate the area's biggest traditional employers, too. Every company is trying to figure out what to do with the Internet. Maybe you have an incredible idea for using the Web as a new distribution channel; if you can find the right person to pitch, you can talk your way into a job you create from whole cloth.

If the company you want to work for is located far from home, try pitching them on letting you work remotely (community-organizer positions are ideally suited for this). If you don't mind travel, you could fly in for a few days every month and work at home the rest of the time.

Part of your ability to transform yourself into an Internet person will be your ability to think creatively about problems, so look at the geography challenge as your first test.

Now that you know where potential jobs may be in your immediate or chosen area (answer: just about everywhere), let's dig a little deeper.

Start at Media Metrix (http://www.mediametrix.com) to find the biggest companies in your target category and drill down from there. The beauty of the Internet is that information once relegated to annual reports or industry press releases is readily available to you. Some company research sites we like include:

- CompaniesOnline (http://www.CompaniesOnline.com)

- Hoover's Online (http://www.hoovers.com)

- *Wall Street Journal* Careers (http://www.careers.wsj.com)

- Vault Reports (http://www.vault.com)

- *Forbes* (http://www.forbes.com)

- *Financial Times* (http://www.ft.com)

- Dun & Bradstreet (http://www.dnb.com)

- Monster Board (http://www.monster.com)

Remember to refer back to the sites listed for each of our specialty sections, too.

What you're looking for are the key players, the financial

It's hard to generalize about Internet development outside the United States: Every country and region has different issues, flow of venture capital, governmental restrictions, and penetration/cost of Internet access. However, there's one thing we *do* feel safe saying about Internet job opportunities abroad: Dot-coms elsewhere are at least one to two years behind their U.S. counterparts—and sometimes more than that.

The big advantage for those of you reading this book in Europe, Asia, India, Israel, South Africa, or one of the other rapidly developing areas is that very few people there have any dot-com experience. Just reading this book will make you sound smarter than others applying for the same positions.

What about Canada? It has a flourishing high-tech sector, and the companies are extremely competitive with their U.S. counterparts. The hiring scene there very much mirrors the American experience. However, pure Internet companies have been slower to develop (venture capital has been less forthcoming north of the border), and Canadian Web companies are where U.S. companies were a year or so ago.

No matter what country you live in, learn as much as you can about the local Internet industry. There are Web sites and magazines that cover your area. The major search engines have country-specific versions with lots of Web resources. Most international newspapers have online versions and print inserts with the URLs of local companies. The big U.S. Internet trade magazines and sites have international editions. If you're in a country in a common market like the European Union, don't stop at your own backyard—explore happenings in neighboring countries, too.

Another source of valuable information is venture capital companies within your country's borders: Who are they funding? Their sites are often full of great leads. Many cities abroad also have regular meetings of Internet professionals (First Tuesday is the big one). Go and make some contacts.

health of the company, and some general background. Because Internet firms change so quickly, up-to-date information is crucial. It's a volatile environment, so take the time to go more in-depth, search out any news articles, and get the back story on the company.

This is particularly true for David firms—those small, aggressive companies springing up on the Net landscape like dandelions. There's far more opportunity among these firms—but also more risk. Take Devin's experience, for example. He had an incredible offer from a snazzy Internet start-up, with higher pay and more equity than he could've hoped for. The future looked bright; he had his new Lexus all picked out. Then a disturbing bit of information popped up during his research on the company: An article revealed that one of the principals had been disbarred for unethical practices involving stocks. It was the same guy who had made him the killer offer. Devin wisely turned it down, saving himself potential career damage. Take full advantage of the Internet's vast resources to find out as much as you can. In fact, as you dig deeper, it may be worth paying for the premium information.

See if you can uncover who's on the board of directors. If it's a public company, that information will likely be on the Web site; otherwise, ask during the interview. Hopefully that research will show they have Internet experience and connections or know a lot about their vertical category.

TRADE PUBLICATIONS

There are several excellent trade publications you should become familiar with. They'll get you up to speed on the latest Internet business issues, the big players, and more. These magazines are available at any good newsstand and, naturally, online. New ones, especially digital newsletters, are being launched every day, but our favorites include:

- Business 2.0 (http://www.business2.com)

- The Industry Standard (http://www.thestandard.com)

- Internet World (http://www.internet.com)

- Fast Company (http://www.fastcompany.com)

- Red Herring (http://www.herring.com)

FINDING THE RIGHT CONTACT

We can't stress this enough: No offense to any human resources people out there, but they are very rarely the right contact. They don't have the power to hire you, unless perhaps you're looking for a job in their department, so avoid them if at all possible.

Besides combing the above trade publications, go to your target company's Web site and look through their "About Us" section for names. Once you get a few that you think are in your ballpark, narrow your research by typing the name into a search engine and looking for related news articles.

If the only contact you can find is the CEO, it's perfectly acceptable in Internet culture to reach out to him or her with an e-mail; they'll most likely pass your information along. Or you can simply go the old-fashioned route and call the main number and ask for the person in charge of your area.

Tools and Resources

Let's look at some other resources that have helped many of our friends and colleagues successfully land great jobs. There's no one method we'd recommend over another. In an industry changing as fast as the Internet, there's an increasing number of job-hunting options. Investigate all of the following and incorporate them into your own personal game plan.

HEADHUNTERS

There are basically two kinds of executive search firms: retained search firms, which get about a third of the salary to fill (typically high-level) positions, and headhunters, who work strictly on commission. In both cases, the recruiter is not really working for you—the client is the company. Headhunters can certainly provide some opportunities, but they don't owe you a job—or anything else.

One more distinction we should point out: An employment agency is *not* the same thing as a headhunter. These generally deal with lower, entry-level positions. That agency ad for a great-sounding Internet job you see in the Sunday classifieds may involve making a lot of coffee. Move on to the comics, unless you're straight out of school with no Internet background or returning to the workforce with no technical skills. If that's you, one of these administrative positions may be the perfect in. Your days as low person on the totem pole may be short-lived. Busy Internet companies frequently put the receptionist or other grunts to work doing higher-level tasks. Remember that even employment agencies are likely to test your basic computer skills; you'll

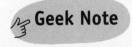 **Geek Note** Getting the e-mail address of your contact may require playing detective. Look at the standard e-mail protocol of your target company: If the HR person's address reads something like jsmith@mail-company.com, you can make a pretty good guess at your contact's e-mail handle.

be expected to have a passable understanding of Microsoft Office Suite before they'll even get you an interview.

Headhunters are increasingly important to Internet companies hungry for talent; many will talk to you even if you have no Internet background. The tricky part is that it's best if they discover *you*, rather than the other way around.

It's a little (actually, a lot) like dating: You want to get their attention, then have them woo you. How to do this? The hands-down best method is an introduction from someone the headhunter has successfully placed. Ask those you know in the business who their headhunter is/was, ask them to call on your behalf or to suggest your name the next time the headhunter is in touch with them (and that will be soon—successful Internet industry execs are inundated with these calls).

The next best method: Attend Internet industry events and do a little networking. If you've done your homework beforehand, you'll know the names of the top recruiters so that you can be on the lookout for the company name on a badge. Casually introduce yourself and mention your skills in a concise, pithy soundbite that they'll remember—but don't beg for a job. Feel free to play the field: One source says that different recruiters have relationships with different companies. It's important to get your name into as many databases as possible.

If you decide to take a chance and contact a headhunter di-

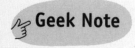 **Geek Note** One of Deborah's favorite front-desk receptionists learned HTML on the job, became a junior— then a senior—producer, *then* left the company to freelance at a very high rate, all within eighteen months!

rectly, get his or her attention with a strong cover letter and a résumé that shows—*specifically*—how your skills will translate to the Internet business environment. Do you have retail experience? They need that in e-commerce positions. If you're a marketing ace, what have you worked on that most closely resembles Internet world issues? One more tip: Don't forget to put your e-mail address on everything; one source says that if that piece of information isn't there, she won't even bother making contact.

When an Internet headhunter agrees to meet with you, he or she is doing it for several reasons: to get a sense of your overall skills and personal qualities but, more important, to see that you're really *ready* to make this change. One expert tells us, "Yes, there's a lot of opportunity in the Internet world—but with that comes risk." The biggest issues she sees among those making the transition are adjusting to the breakneck pace, handling the scope of the work, and learning to work with the technology. How ready and willing are you to roll with these punches? When you're trying to convince a headhunter that you're a great candidate for them to shop to an Internet firm, a realistic, can-do attitude will help soften your lack of experience.

Be up front about what it is you're looking for—and what you absolutely won't consider. Is anything longer than a one-hour commute out of the question? Let the recruiter know your limits early in the process, but recognize the difference between being specific and being inflexible: A new hire is unlikely to be able to snag a corner office, six-figure salary, and threeday workweek. (If you find such a place, let us know. Now!)

When it comes to the actual interview, one headhunting guru counsels her candidates to get past the No Experience thing by going into the meeting *really* well prepared. This means doing your homework on the company, spending a lot of time thinking about the business and the specific skills you can offer. "If you do that," she says, "they'll notice, and you'll be miles ahead of the others."

Once a headhunter picks you up on the radar, he or she can certainly open the door to some Internet opportunities, but that's no guarantee it'll be a perfect fit. You'll still need to do your own due diligence. Again, remember that *the headhunter does not work for you.* Don't let anyone push you into a position that doesn't feel right—there are plenty of other opportunities out there.

And don't be overly tempted by every opportunity a recruiter floats your way. Sure, you can leverage an offer from a new firm into a better deal with your current employer—even a *rumor* that a headhunter has approached you can have that effect in a tight labor market. Poaching is a fact of life in the business, but use it too often and you'll be tagged a blackmailer. One executive says he turned down a great candidate after seeing he'd been placed by a search firm one time too many: It seemed he would forever be jumping to the next competitor who waved money around.[1] There are more ethical ways to get a raise.

NEWSGROUPS

Newsgroups can be a useful tool in your search. Essentially a discussion forum, you and fellow members "post" and "reply to" messages (or "threads") about a specific topic—such as a certain job category. This can include leads, battle stories, or other information. Frequently, you can request that information be automatically e-mailed to you.

Newsgroups won't necessarily land you an interview (although

---

1. Stephen M. Pollan with Mark Levine, "This Means War," *Worth,* October 1999, p. 109.

stranger things have happened), but these forums do allow you to follow marketplace trends and salaries, make contacts, and get advice and feedback from those who work in a specialty or company you're looking at.

You can find a newsgroup via any standard search engine, or at career Web sites like Hot Jobs, Monster Board, and Career Mosaic.

Many job-related newsgroups are meant for job seekers only, but it may prove to be the way into a headhunter's database. Many recruiters actively seek potential candidates here. Says one, "I may not necessarily post a job opening to the list, but I do pay attention to what people say in response to questions that are posed, and that's more likely how I suss them out."[2]

Online bulletin boards are a variation on this theme: A topic is posted and people respond to it. Sometimes actual running conversations may start, but generally, it's a lot of on-off replies.

It's certainly worth checking the online bulletin boards of colleges, alumni associations, and, of course, any company you're in-

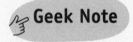 **Geek Note** A word of caution about newsgroups and mailing lists: they frequently have a virtual life of their own. You may only be casually or temporarily interested in the topic at hand, but there may be dozens, even hundreds, of online diehards ready to pick up any message thread. When one of Deborah's former colleagues left the company, his e-mail was forwarded to Deborah. Turns out he had forgotten to unsubscribe from one group that generated an average of seventy-five e-mails a day. When you're done with a newsgroup, remember to remove your name from the mailing list.

2. Lisa Hamm-Greenwalt, "No Food, but Good Networking at Net Forums," *Internet World*, April 26, 1999, p. 34.

terested in to dig up potential Internet job leads. And don't forget the boards you'll find at the job sites.

JOB SITES

There are hundreds of employment-related Web sites, all which promise to hook you up with your perfect employer. See "Resources" for a more complete listing, but some of those sites are Monster.com, Jobs.com, and America's Job Bank. Many of these focus on traditional jobs, although Internet-related opportunities of the nontechnical kind can appear. You should also check out:

- http://www.atnewyork.com
Good market intelligence on the industry, particularly New York–based companies; has a great newsletter everyone should subscribe to, no matter where they live.

- http://www.nynma.org
The New York New Media Association; has terrific jobs board and lists all the events worth knowing about in NYC.

- http://www.norcalcompanies.com
Directory of companies in northern California; good resource for finding the basic info on firms; you have to pay to get more.

- http://www.bayarea.com
The *San Jose Mercury News* is the local newspaper for Silicon Valley; this site covers news on companies and activities there.

- http://www.siliconvalleycareers.com
Good spot to find out all about California-based high-tech employers.

- http://webworkwhere.com
Internet companies around the country.

One of the technical pros we spoke with says that an increasing number of headhunters and large companies use data-mining software to comb these sites in search of bodies. You don't have much control over who might see your information (like your current boss); but if you don't care, post it wherever you can. A software program might just pick you up (see Geek Note on p. 204).

The days when you searched the want ads, dug some information out of a few out-of-date trade journals, and hoped that you and the company would be a good match are pretty much over. A wealth of "insider" resources await you on the Internet, which will help you sidestep the wrong company and zero in on the right one for you.

You've lined up your targets; now let's hit 'em with all barrels—there are more than two in the digital world.

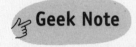 **Geek Note**

One tech expert says a growing number of companies use automation software to scan résumés for certain qualifications. Help yourself rise to the top of the pile by using keywords that the computer will pick up, in both your cover letter and your résumé: *sales, marketing, business development,* and so on. And because most search engines aren't smart enough to differentiate between your past experience and what you *want* to do, feature the keywords *Internet* and *experience* in your "Objective" body copy.

Chapter 13

HUNTING LESSONS
The Best Ways to Bag Your Internet Prey

As you saw in the last chapter, there are many, many ways to dig up great Internet career opportunities. Now you need to capture the attention of the right people at those companies and convince them to hire you, even if you don't have prior Internet experience.

Now for our own FAQ list:

DO I NEED MY OWN WEB PAGE?

This question comes up a lot and the answer is . . . no, no, and *no!* Unless you're a designer (in which case a personal page is a must), you absolutely *do not* need a Web page to impress a potential Internet boss. And the truth is, one that's poorly executed or out of date will do more harm than good. Spend your time and energy creating a good résumé—one that looks neat not just in hard copy, but also when it's transmitted electronically.

WHAT SHOULD BE ON MY RÉSUMÉ?

If you haven't updated your résumé in a while, it's worth looking at a few books or career sites like Monster.com for fresh tips on formatting and other issues. Remember that although you'll need hard copies, in all likelihood you'll be sending your résumé digitally, so don't get carried away with complicated fonts and graphics. They'll only be lost or, worse, translate as a horrendous mess when you send it via e-mail. You may also be asked to cut-and-paste your information into the body of an e-mail, rather than attaching it as a file; ask which method is preferred.

Microsoft Word is the preferred format. Save your cover letter and résumé as a text or *.txt file, or a plain ASCII file, and *make sure your name is in the title of that file* (JaneSmithresume.txt). The people you're pitching get dozens of e-mail attachments every week with the hopelessly generic name of resume.doc. Don't let yours get lost in the pile.

Your résumé should include your name, address, and home phone number (where you better have an answering machine or voice mail). Include a work number *only* if you're in a position to have conversations with your prospective employer from your current office. One more thing: Do *not* give a cell phone number unless you leave it on at all times and are prepared to answer it.

Naturally, an e-mail address is key. We reiterate the importance of having a private, non-location-specific address *outside* of your company: Look into Hotmail, Yahoo! Mail, or Netscape—or even the service offered on your favorite site. And although it may seem obvious, remember to check this account as regularly as your others!

You'll want either a concise job objective or professional summary section at the top of the first page. Generally, we find *objectives* more appropriate when you're going after a specific job; a *summary* is more effective if you're not sure who'll see your résumé or what positions are currently available at the company. The beauty of the digital age is that you can easily customize these elements for every time you send out your résumé. Remember, too, our tips on using keywords like *Internet*, *sales*, or *marketing*, which résumé-scanning software is often programmed to pick up (see Geek Note on p. 204).

"Short and sweet" is the guiding tenet of the Internet. Because you have nanoseconds to get the average Internet exec's attention, the top one-third of your résumé is critical. So put the meat up front and keep it to one page if possible. Two is the absolute limit—learn to edit your experience on paper. And spell-check: There is absolutely no excuse for typos.

Because you have no Internet background, how do you tantalize the digital world with your skills? Think in terms of *results, results, results.* You want to communicate clearly how what you've done in your career thus far will translate into the Internet space: What projects did you initiate? Did you exceed any goals? What did you create or implement? What new ideas did you come up with? It's an *extremely* results-oriented medium, so wherever possible, use active words like *created, initiated,* and *developed.* Also, the Internet loves people who think big, so add real numbers and percentages wherever you can: "increased sales 200 percent," "managed a $20-million advertising budget," etc. Emphasize good tenure on previous jobs; one executive recruiter reads that as in indication of loyalty, a scarce commodity in the Internet world.

Mention your education and any professional certifications you have. While you're at it, consider joining local Internet organizations (see "Resources" for some listings). You'll learn something, meet new people, and show initiative to a prospective employer.

HOW CAN I BEST USE E-MAIL IN MY JOB SEARCH?

In the frantic pace of the digital world, cold calls over the telephone from a job hunter (you) are about as welcome as an *E. coli* outbreak. However, cold e-mails are usually okay.

Remember that there's a genuine fear and loathing of spam—

not to mention computer viruses—so industry people are very cautious about opening e-mail from a sender they don't recognize. Use your subject line to let them know this isn't one more piece of junk e-mail. If you're applying for a specific job, mention it in the heading. If you share a mutual acquaintance, use that name ("Joe Smith suggested I write . . ."). Of course, this applies only if Joe Smith actually *did* suggest it; if your connection to Joe is somewhat more tenuous, be circumspect in using his name.

If you don't have a connection or a specific job in mind, be creative and tantalize them with the contents of your subject line. Make them think they have something to gain by opening your message. However, don't be so creative you deceive them: "What a cool business model" or "Loved your comments in *Internet World*" will get you further than "You've won a million dollars!" which has "trash me" written all over it.

Internet industry executives use e-mail as one of their main forms of communication and are inundated every single day. Be considerate and keep your message *extremely* brief. Use bullet points to tell them who you are and what your interest in their company is; then ask for what you want: a meeting in person, if possible. You can be a little bit pushy, particularly if your research convinces you there's a good fit for you at this company. If this idea makes you uncomfortable, remember there are never enough hands on deck in most Internet companies. Your getting in touch

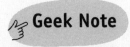 **Geek Note** While you can certainly give your résumé a "tech makeover" yourself, there are some great online services that will take it on for you (for a fee). Resume.com, for example, uses templates that will trigger the most desirable keywords on job sites like monster.com. Worth investigating, we'd say.

with them may actually help them solve a staffing problem. We know one person hired for a VP job simply because she sent an e-mail to the right person on the right day.

Even if you've found the right contact (as we outlined in the previous chapter), there are no guarantees your e-mail will be answered. Here's what could happen to your unsolicited e-mail message:

- The person never opens it.

- The person opens it, but doesn't respond because he or she (1) is too busy, (2) forgot, (3) doesn't really need anyone right now.

- The person opens it, but doesn't think you're a good fit.

- The person forwards it to someone else in the company, who either doesn't open it or puts it into categories 1, 2, or 3 above.

- The person responds, or the person it was forwarded to responds, and you get your meeting!

The worst possible outcome is to have your message forwarded to the human resources department. *You do not want to talk to the human resources department first.* Usually, all they can do is screen you out or play gatekeeper to the real interview—they simply can't offer you the job you want. However, if after all your dig-

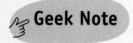 **Geek Note** Memorize this: *Short and sweet* is the hallmark of digital behavior. The environment is crazy, so from memos to e-mails to meetings, learn to make your point quickly. But check that your spelling and punctuation are correct.

ging, HR is the only contact you can locate, go for it. It's still better than nothing.

So now you're waiting to hear back. And waiting. And maybe waiting some more. If you haven't heard back in ten days, by all means send your e-mail again. Remember, they likely didn't respond because they were simply too busy; by politely reminding them that they didn't respond, you're showing your interest and persistence.

Be clear in your subject line, concise in your message. Something along the lines of "Just wanted to follow up on the message I sent last week regarding my interest in your company. Again, my qualifications are as follows . . ." goes over far better than "Why the #$!#* haven't you responded to my letter?!"

If, after that, you *still* don't hear from them, drop it and move on. If you have a personal contact at that company, you might want to enlist his or her help in finding out what's up; but if not, don't be a pest. There's a big world out there to explore.

WHAT ARE THE RULES FOR NETWORKING ONLINE?

The Netiquette of online schmoozing with newsgroups or mailing lists is pretty analogous to the way you'd conduct yourself at any industry cocktail party: Stick to the topic and be willing to share information, articles, and contacts that might be helpful to

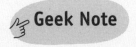 **Geek Note** What if you're pregnant? Pitch via e-mail and phone as much as possible. If you're good, you'll get the interview; and they'll probably like you so much, they'll hire you, and you can start off working from home during your maternity leave. Get the interview, then worry about it.

some or all of the members (remember, what goes around, comes around). If someone's offered to help with a specific piece of information by providing a contact name, thank them with a prompt and courteous e-mail both before and after. However, don't overdo it: Follow-up is one thing, but don't abuse your e-mail privileges with a daily "what's up?" inquiry.

Don't forget to do plenty of "offline" networking as well. There are basically six degrees of separation in this young business; it seems that everyone knows someone else. Hunt down every connection you can possibly think of, show up at job fairs, event parties, and send cordial e-mails to people who you think are doing interesting things in the business. With all these avenues—digital and otherwise—to exploit, it won't be long before you land an interview. And probably, more than one!

GO!

Woo-hoo! All your homework has paid off big—you've landed an interview with your dream Internet company! After the initial adrenaline rush wears off, you may find yourself asking, "Now what?" In this section, we'll focus on that out-of-body experience more commonly known as . . . The Interview.

First is an overview of what you should know beforehand and what to expect when you get there. Then we'll take you through the time-honored dance of clinching the deal and getting your share of the virtual pie.

By the end of this section, your confidence will be soaring because you'll know:

- The key questions to ask to look really smart.

- How to spin your previous, non-Internet career to the best advantage.

- The perks and benefits most commonly available at a dot-com—and how to make sure you get the ones you want.

- How to avoid asking for the wrong things—and what those wrong things are.

- How to navigate the stock-options maze: What it all means, what's valuable, what's just smoke and mirrors.

- How to figure out if this company is for real.

Take a few deep breaths before you settle into that uncomfortable chair across from the head honcho's desk—we'll help you come out the other side a winner!

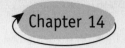

Chapter 14

THE MAIN EVENT
The Sweaty Palm Factor

Congratulations, you've got an appointment! Get your sharp-est black outfit out of the dry cleaners; here's the prep work to do beforehand, plus tips on what to expect during the actual one-on-one.

You've already done your homework on the company. As one expert headhunter advises, the better prepared you are going into a meeting, the easier it will be for your interviewer(s) to overlook your lack of prior Internet experience.

You should know:

- What the company does: are they an e-commerce site, con-tent, B2B, what? Review chapter 1 on business models. Go to the company's Web site and read the mission statement. If it doesn't have one or it's not available, prepare some questions to ask about the company's goals.

- How successful is it? The trades and corporate press releases will give you some idea, but you'll want to ask point-blank, too.

- Is it a David or a Goliath in the Internet world? How old is the company? How quickly is it growing?

- Who's on the board? Who are the key players in the company? Research the principals by name whenever possible (very important, particularly with a start-up!).

- Who funded the company?

- Who are its competitors and where does it fit in the competitive marketplace?

Log on and dig up the most recent news about the company, its competitors, and its industry in general. Talk to anyone you know who knows anything about the company or its business in general. If it's an e-commerce firm, learn about competitors who sell the same categories of merchandise in the brick-and-mortar world. Take advantage of all the information available to you, both online and offline, and show the company you're someone who "thinks beyond the job." These are the kind of people who thrive in the Internet business.

After your research, you should have a pretty good idea what this company is all about, so let's fast-forward to the interview.

The interview process at an Internet firm can differ significantly from that at a traditional workplace. First, don't be surprised if you're asked to sign a nondisclosure agreement (NDA) before the interview starts or even before it's scheduled; in the ferociously competitive Internet world, information is precious

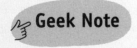 **Geek Note** Although you probably submitted your résumé electronically, it's entirely possible your contact hasn't gotten around to printing out hard copies. Bring a few with you.

and no one wants you walking off and blabbing about his or her intellectual property at your next interview.

Your interview is likely to be faster and more intense than any you've experienced in the "real" world. Instead of being brought back for a second round, you may meet various managers and staff in the course of one visit. Consider it a very good sign if the person interviewing you abruptly stops and picks up the phone or wanders off down the hall looking for someone else they want you to meet. That means you've passed their "smell test" and they want someone else to confirm that you're a good candidate. This is a great chance for you to find out more about the management team: Ideally, you'll learn that at least one or two senior people understand the Internet, and that at least some of them have experience in their vertical category so that the company's not spending time reinventing the wheel.

Of course, halfway through the interview, your host may decide you're not the right person for the job—but there's *another* position you'd be perfect for and you'll have to talk to someone else. This is a pretty likely scenario for someone with little or no Internet experience: Your background might be perfect for *something*, but only the folks inside the cubicles know what that project is.

This whirlwind process gives you a snapshot of the company—and a chance for both of you to see if there's a good fit. Things change constantly in this business, and if you're easily thrown off-balance during a fast-paced interview, it's good that your interviewer—and you—find that out early on.

Another thing to remember is that the person on the other side of the desk may very well be younger and less experienced than you. And you can bet that his or her expertise is not in conducting job interviews. Use that to your advantage, moving the interview forward in a direction that favors *you* and makes you look smart and capable.

Use the opportunity to size up the interviewer, because it's likely he or she will be your supervisor. How is the interviewer conducting himself or herself? Has he or she shown you the courtesy of letting the phone ring to voice mail during the interview? Or is the interviewer being interrupted every few minutes and checking e-mail as you respond to a question?

In each of our specialty chapters, we covered the questions you're likely to be asked about particular jobs. Here are some general ones that may also come up during the grilling process:

- What do you do in your current job?

- Does your present company use the Internet? How?

- Why do you want to change jobs?

- What are your strengths and weaknesses?

- How do you deal with change?

- Why do you want to work in an Internet business?

- How do you use the Internet?

- What sites do you regularly visit and why?

- What do you think of our company's Web site? (Have some solid, yet diplomatic, observations.)

- Have you bought anything online? What and who from?

- What special skills do you have (software, etc.)?

- How do you do working in a chaotic, unstructured environment?

- Have you thought about the contributions you could make to this firm?

And here's a biggie: What's unique about you? What can you bring to the party?

This is where you can demonstrate that, even if you've never worked in the Internet business before, you "get it." What interviewers look for with this particular question are things that make them feel you'll fit. It's your chance to highlight professional assets that can add to or balance their existing skill set—a strong background in retailing is a big plus when you're interviewing with an e-commerce company, for example. Here's where you can also share personal interests that would add spice to (or balance) the mix.

Cindy, for example, has an interest in holistic health (amazing, considering how much diet Coke we both inhaled in the course of writing this book). When one of her clients wanted to build a Web site on that topic, she let them know she read widely on the subject. The combination of her writing skills and personal passion for the subject landed her a job as editor of the site. Think of your own outside interests or experiences and what they can add to the company's mission.

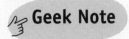 **Geek Note** The company needs you to hit the ground running, so don't ever say "I'm here to learn" during the interview. They need to at least *think* you're going to be independent and self-sufficient. Even if they really will have to train you, don't rub their noses in it—it won't help your cause.

You may have to be aggressive in steering the conversation to the areas you want to cover. This is particularly true if you're interviewing with someone less experienced: He or she may do all the talking! That takes the pressure off of you, but at some point you need to determine if this is the right place for you. When you see your chance, take the bull by the horns and talk about yourself. Then ask about the following:

THE BUSINESS PLAN

What's the company trying to accomplish? You've already studied its business model in the information-gathering stage—now make them say what it is they want to do (and hope it's more specific than "make a ton of money, then sell it to the first big portal that comes along").

If the company is very much in start-up mode, ask to see its *actual* business plan or at least the presentation kit they're walking around with. This will give you a pretty fair indication of who they are and whether their idea is solid. Make sure what they tell you is consistent with what you've read. If not, find out why you're hearing one thing from the company and something else from the press. If there is wild inconsistency, you may have uncovered a big problem: Run, don't walk, away from this job.

Follow up with some questions that show you understand the business, such as:

- Has your business model stayed the same since the inception of the company?

- If it's changed, what's different? How did you arrive at the decision to change?

- Where are the growth areas in the company? What's "booming"?

- Do you have plans to establish additional revenue streams? What are they? Who's responsible for that?

- Do you work with other Internet companies? How?

- How are the company's goals disseminated and made a reality? Via meetings, memos, what?

- How is the company organized? (Hope that they have or can draw you an org chart that makes sense.)

- What kind of budget will I have? And what do you expect from it? (If you're interviewing for a marketing job with a $50,000 budget and they expect you to deliver an audience as large as the one that watches the Super Bowl, be somewhat skeptical.)

By the way, if the business plan is contingent on a single big partnership or deal, make sure that it's a done one. You don't want to be in the position one of our sources found herself in when the "partner" never came through and the doors were closed on her new job shortly after she'd started.

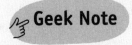 **Geek Note**   During the interview, don't be so blunt as to ask, "What's your exit strategy?" This is akin to asking "How much money do you make, and by the way, what are your sexual preferences?" Although many Internet companies *do* have a predetermined exit strategy—such as going public or being acquired by a bigger firm—and a clear schedule for implementing it, you get at that information by asking bigger questions about the business model and how they think the landscape and opportunities will evolve.

FUNDING

Where is the money coming from and is there more where it came from? An early stage company may be funded by the founder's credit cards, by angel investors (read "parents"), or by early stage investors. If you're interviewing at such a firm, ask these questions—the answers may mean the difference between a paycheck that bounces and one that doesn't.

If the firm is a David backed by venture capitalists, who are those investors? How many rounds of financing have there been? How close is the next round, and how sure a thing is it? What percent of the company do the founders and employees have, and how much do the VCs own? Some of the top venture-capital firms include Flatiron Partners, Draper Fisher Jurvetson, Hummer Winblad, and Benchmark. These firms often network their portfolio of investments and send business from one to another. (You might want to take a quick look back at chapter 1 for a primer on the funding dance.)

On the subject of money, try to gauge just what they're spending their dough on: A company with responsible management, for example, won't blow funding on fancy remodeling of an office that's already clean, safe, and well-connected to the Internet, or on endless pricey lunches. If it does, that's a pretty good sign that the executives haven't made the adjustment to the bare-bones mentality required of a growing Internet firm. You don't want a job at a place that's going to plow through the money before the company can really take off.

CORPORATE CULTURE

You may think the Internet is all T-shirts and blue jeans, but that's not universally true—particularly in the Goliath firms and in companies serving the business. It's unlikely that an Internet firm will be as button-down as a bank, but they may still prefer a sports coat and slacks over cutoffs and sandals. Or maybe they don't care. Find out so you won't be embarrassed when you show up on your first day looking like you're headed to a funeral—it just happens to be Hawaiian Shirt Day.

As Internet companies compete both with each other and with brick-and-mortar companies to keep employees happy, you'll find a dizzying array of benefits and perks. Ask about them. At one firm, a Foosball table located a little too close to Deborah's work-space made it tough for her to have quiet business conversations. But Foosball was part of the deal for the junior designers, so she learned to shut her door and live with it.

Another company brought breakfast in every Monday as sort of a welcome to the new week, then had beer and pretzels on Friday afternoons. Every firm is different. The Goliaths in particular have created some wacky and fun rituals to keep the employees happy, but you'll want to know about the less wacky ones like emergency child-care arrangements, new employee orientation, and car service for those late nights at the office.

One more key question: Is the position located at the company headquarters or at an outpost? For your first Internet job, try to be where the action is. You may eventually get promoted to run the London office, but to learn anything, you need to be on site in the early going.

THE WORKING STYLE

Flexibility is one of the hallmarks of the Internet industry. If the ability to work at home or have flex hours is critical to you, then by all means, bring it up with your potential supervisor relatively early in the interview process. However, our advice is not to focus on these issues *too* early; instead try to get a feel for the company's position on them first (the only exception here is for someone going for a community position, where working at home is the norm; see chapter 9).

Get the job offer in hand and *then* negotiate. It would be very unusual for an Internet company to retract an offer if you tell them that you need to be home by three o'clock on Thursdays to coach your kid's soccer team—as long as you commit to working those extra hours somehow (the next chapter deals more specifically with the kinds of benefits and perks you can negotiate).

Once you prove your worth to a company, almost anything is possible. One employee we know had an idea for a new start-up but he wasn't ready to quit his existing job. He worked out a deal to maintain his current salary but work only thirty hours per week. He got the time he craved to work on his own project and the company was happy to hold on to a valued employee.

BUT ENOUGH ABOUT ME

At any point in the conversation, it's appropriate, and recommended, to ask about *them*. The people in this business have diverse backgrounds, great stories, and a passion for the industry that they're all too happy to share. It's not just ego stroking; you really will learn something by turning the spotlight on your interviewer.

Getting the Offer

The interview is moving along. You and the boss are really clicking, and you can envision working in the next cubicle. The questions have all been asked and answered, and now all that's left is for you to shake hands, say thanks, and wait for the e-mail offering you the job. It may play out that way, but we're here to tell you that in the virtual world, things move *really* fast, which means, it's okay to ask for the job right then and there.

First, a few provisos. If you're at all uncertain about accepting the job, don't push (warning signs: If one or more of their answers makes you uneasy, or if you're just trying to get the offer to leverage your current job). But if you feel relatively certain that you'd take the job if they offered it (at the right salary, bonus, options, etc.), then go ahead and ask.

The worst you'll get is a "let us get back to you." Believe us, in the busy world of the Internet, the last thing that person you're talking to wants to do is to keep looking. If you like them and they like you, go for it!

The real negotiation for the salary, bonus, and options usually comes after you and the employer have both decided that you're the right person for the job. The hardest part was making the match; it's rare for a deal to fall apart over the details.

One thing to remember when you're interviewing: The com-

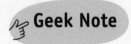 **Geek Note** Several Internet veterans offered this unusual advice: If you're still unsure about a move to the digital world, try before you buy. One company encourages potential hires to literally sit in their new workspace for two or three days before they accept the job. Another company requires new hires at every level to trail one of their peers for the first day or two, sitting in on phone calls and meetings to get a feel for how they do business. Because most Internet employers probably won't suggest this great idea on their own, make it happen for yourself! Of course, they may want to test-drive you, too, by requesting a project or some homework before anything's official. Use your judgment: You don't want to do work for free, but it may be worth it to give everyone some peace of mind about the fit.

petitive, job-hopping world of the Internet has spawned a cocky, what-can-you-do-for-me? attitude in some job seekers (especially younger, less-experienced ones). Demand for talent is high, time is short, and everyday people are becoming better negotiators. Still, the best advice is to tread lightly. "I've seen people push more and more. It turns me off," says the CEO of one staffing firm.[1] Even with the informal atmosphere of the high-tech world, play it safe by not demanding too much too soon. Stick to old-fashioned etiquette.

No matter what the response is, immediately send a digital thank-you note. Miss Manners may be rolling her eyes, but as one human resources director notes, "The process in total has gotten less formal."[2] Many things may be changing in the virtual world, but common courtesy isn't one of them.

A speedy follow-up is not just courteous but could make the difference between whether you get an offer or not. As one of our sources emphasized, "If he or she doesn't call me or send me an e-mail immediately afterward, I'm not interested."

That said, proceed to the next chapter to negotiate a killer deal for yourself!

---

1. Stephanie Armour, "Anything Goes in Age of e-Mail, Employee Auctions, Khaki Fridays," *bizreport.com*, November 26, 1999.
2. Ibid.

☞ OUR COMPLETELY SUBJECTIVE LIST OF POSSIBLE SIGNS THAT YOU MAY NOT WANT TO WORK FOR A COMPANY

* If the founder or founders have no experience in the Internet business, the vertical of their product or site, or managing any group of people . . . ever.

* No one will tell you where the next round of money is coming from (probably because no one knows).

* The business plan is so ambitious, it's un-doable. This is different than thinking big: You want the founders to think big but have realistic plans.

* There's high turnover that no one has a good explanation for. Try to track down one of the fleeing employees and find out "whassup."

* You walk in off the street with no Internet experience, and they offer to rewrite the organizational chart to create a job for you. No offense, but why are they so desperate?

* If the company seems to have been founded for no better reason than to make the founders rich. Someone there better have a genuine passion for the product or Web site. Getting rich is not enough.

* The business plan is fixated on numbers and research rather than what's going on in the market. Someone needs to reality-check it all.

* The board of directors or advisers is made up of people who aren't going to help the business. That could mean relatives of the founders or original angel investors. What you'd like to see are some people on the board who can contribute to the success of the enterprise.

* Another corollary: If the founders have given up control of their company to get funding, who's making the decisions about the future of the firm and what are their real motivations? If VCs are running the board, for example, they could sell the company out from under the founders without their consent—or shutter it entirely.

Chapter 15

SUCH A DEAL
Ask for What You Really Want!

Why do you want to make the leap into the wired world? To advance your career? Get on the fast track? Find an outlet for your creativity? Make things happen at the speed of light? All good, and we hope you believe in some of them, but admit it: One of the big draws is the potential to strike it rich. Internet firms desperate for qualified people are working this and every other angle they can to get you on board.

Besides the promise of future riches, the work world of the new economy offers great opportunities for things like telecommuting and flex time. There may also be more unusual companywide perks—everything from free food to neck massages. As you negotiate a deal, here's what's realistic and how to best work it to your advantage.

We caution you to tread lightly here. If the company has a predetermined package of perks, don't be *too* nitpicky. You do *not* want to come off as high maintenance, especially at this early stage of your Internet career. If you're too demanding, they could retract the offer. It's happened.

Salaries

Although we can't provide specifics, salaries among most Internet firms are generally competitive; check the related chapter on your specialty for more guidance. When it comes to things like bonuses and commissions, however, the ball is in your court. These can be largely negotiable, and that includes signing bonuses. Although they're less common for those new to the industry, if you think you can get one, ask!

Equity

The phrase *stock options* has become a mantra in the Internet world. A report from PricewaterhouseCoopers reveals that Internet firms use equity as an enticement to keep staff on board far more than brick-and-mortar companies do.[1] And with takes about dot-com grunts who became fabulously wealthy after their company went public, you can see the appeal.

According to the National Center for Employee Ownership, the number of U.S. workers with access to company stock options increased from one million in 1992 to about eight million in 1999.[2] All of these employee-owners are hoping they'll strike it rich, too. But before you're completely blinded by those dollar signs, keep in mind that there *are no guarantees*: The Internet is an entrepreneurial hotbed and, as such, can be very speculative. Still, in the spirit of optimism, here are the basics.

 **Geek Note**

LEGAL DISCLAIMER
We've been as thorough as we can here—but options are very complicated things. What follows is in no way definitive comprehensive advice. We urge you to consult your own attorney or tax consultant about any offer you may be considering.

1. "Firms Rely on Stock Deals to Keep Staff," *BizReport.com*, November 15, 1999.
2. Michael Chaffers, "Negotiating Stock Options Packages," *Monster.com*, January 2000.

When a company incorporates, they decide who owns what, issuing shares in that company. The founders and top executives obviously try to keep as much of the pie for themselves as possible. One of our sources says that generally, the CEO may have up to 10 percent, the most valued officers will be offered anywhere between 2 and 4 percent, and VPs from 0.5 to 2 percent. Then there are angel investors and/or venture capitalists who invest money in return for a stake in the company. They get shares, too.

When other employees are hired, they're not usually issued actual shares; instead they're given *options* to purchase a certain number of shares at a designated price (and with numerous restrictions). This price is called the *strike price*. You may get rich if the strike price is significantly lower than the market value of the share, when the company goes public and the shares are traded for many times the strike price, or if the company is bought and a takeover price-per-share results. Remember, though—it's all speculative.

From the employer's standpoint, options are another way to pay you without forking over any real money. Every option-holder has a stake in the success of the company (and because you get more over time, it's an incentive for you to stick with the company). The ultimate value of a stock option is almost impossible to determine because it depends heavily on factors that are largely out of your control. For this reason, experts advise you *not* to think of them as cash in hand: options are not your excuse to go out and buy a Porsche.

There are two kinds of employee stock option. *Nonqualified* are most common. When you exercise (or cash in) your options, you'll be taxed on the difference between what you pay for the share (the strike price) and what it's worth in the market.

Incentive stock options are much more attractive taxwise. If you hold on to your options, purchase and then hold the shares for a requisite period of time, your profits will be taxed only at the (usually lower) capital gains tax rate. Unfortunately, ISOs are less commonly offered to new employees.

In *both* cases, you'll pay tax on the difference between the market value from the day you converted your option into a share and the price when you sell that share in the market.

Even the earliest-stage company will typically have a stock-option plan; it's a standard business document the lawyers churn out when the company incorporates. Make sure you get a copy and understand the particulars (once again, talk to your lawyer or accountant).

All options aren't created equal. Typically, shares for employees are part of a pool. How much is in that pool and what do your shares represent? For example, ten thousand shares may seem like a lot—but if there are one hundred million in the pool, it's not so impressive.

The strike price is the big variable here. That's the price at which you can eventually buy your shares, thus exercising your option. Public companies issue shares at market price, but for private companies in the midst of the funding dance, it's much harder to determine the value. Timing is everything here: The earlier you get in the game, the lower the strike price will be on the option. This is because the company is valued at less early on, so each share is worth less. However, if you arrive at a company right on the eve of an IPO, the strike price may be right around the market price of the initial offering—which doesn't leave you much of a chance to make a profit. This may also be true for a mature Internet company, like Yahoo! or AOL. The best you can do is to track the company's stock history to get a very rough sense of what the stock *may* do down the road (operative word: *may*).

One of the other big pieces of the options puzzle is a little thing called vesting. This is how long you have to work at the company before you have the right to exercise the options. Most Internet firms generally work on a four-year cycle, which means after your first year, 25 percent of your options vest, and the other 75 percent vest equally over the next three years. However, with such heated movement in the Internet world, some are offering *monthly* vesting after your first year with them. And in some cases, the cycle is shortening.

Another factor that can dramatically affect your shares' worth is called a *lockup*. After the stock goes public, insiders and venture backers are not permitted to sell their shares until a predetermined period of time has passed, usually 180 days. During that time, their shares cannot be put up for sale; however, when the deal is finalized and the investors give the green light, insiders and backers can unload their shares, potentially flooding the market and thus causing the overall value to drop. To control the impact, some companies stagger the schedule on which the shares are released. Barring this, one expert says that if the number of shares coming public is less than ten times the amount of supply currently trading, you should be okay.[3]

When it comes to getting a better feel for your options, you won't be out of line if you ask these questions:

- Is the company an LLC or a corporation? (If the answer is LLC, talk to a lawyer; everything listed below really only applies to a corporation.)

- How many shares has the company issued up to now?

---

3. Kimberly Weisul, "Firms Seek to Extend Lockups," *Interactive Week*, February 7, 2000, p. 68.

- What is the percent of shares allocated to the employee option pool?

- What percentage of the employee pool am I getting?

- Are there opportunities to earn additional options?

- What has happened historically to the strike prices?

- What is the vesting schedule?

- Is there a lock-up period?

- What happens to the stock options if our company is purchased? (Options should vest on an accelerated schedule in that case.)

- Is the number of options I can expect predetermined, or is there room to negotiate?

- And the big question: Are you planning to issue more shares soon? Do you know how many more? What valuation does that put on the outstanding shares?

Your part of the pool could become seriously diluted when the company goes back to the financial community for an additional round of investment. New shares will be issued, which means that your holdings are now a smaller percentage of the whole. That's good and bad: Your stake may be smaller, but the investors will set a value on each share that's usually higher than the previous round—so your options are theoretically worth more.

It's unlikely, but ask if your company's plan has an "antidilution" provision, which automatically issues employees additional shares during funding rounds to keep things stable. If it doesn't, console yourself with the fact that you could *still* end up with a piece—even if it's smaller—of a much bigger company. Besides, if the company didn't get the funding, your options would be worth zero because you'd all be out of business.

The other key to understanding the value of your options is to know where the company is in the development process. If it's already gone public, the chance to get in on the really cheap strike price and turn it into gold is probably over. If the company is red hot and goes public, your strike price (generally the trading price on the day the option is awarded) could still be much lower than where the stock is going. Who knows?

We know one batch of employees who joined a company shortly after it went public. The stock was skyrocketing, and options were awarded at multiples of three to four times the IPO price. But then (you know what's coming) the stock plummeted, leaving their options extremely unattractive (who wants an option to buy a share at $50 when the market price is $15?). That's when your options are said to be "underwater," basically worthless unless the stock price goes back up. Companies in this situation will frequently issue new blocks of options at the lower strike price to encourage these understandably frustrated employees to stay. If the price goes back up, those employees might be back in the money.

For these unpredictable reasons, it's always wise to consider options as gravy. If you're taking a pay cut and hoping that options will one day make up for it, a good rule of thumb is to ask for a salary that at least covers your expenses, with an options package that will outweigh that salary gap. For example, if you're agreeing to take a 10 percent salary cut, ask for anywhere from 15 to 20 percent of your current salary in options.[4]

Companies can tempt you with options talk all they want, but *more* doesn't always mean *better*: If you're lucky enough to be

---

4. Sean Donahue, "Run the Option Play," *Business 2.0*, January 2000, p. 238.

weighing several offers, embrace your Inner Venture Capitalist and take a hard look at each company's prospects: the track record of the founders, the viability of the business model and growth rate, the competition, and which investors and board members have signed on. Here's one sobering fact to keep in mind: For every ten companies that offer employees options packages, only one ever goes public.[5]

And because options plans can be daunting to slog through, once again, *consult a lawyer or financial planner*. To get the most out of your options, *you'll* have to take the bull by the horns and learn what you need to know—less than a third of companies offering options distribute comprehensive information about them to their staff.[6] There are a lot of folks out there who unwittingly let their options expire or who didn't think they could afford to purchase their shares. And there are plenty of people who made bad career decisions based on speculative options plans. Don't become one of them.

Bonuses and Perks

In the Internet world, you can't count on that nice end-of-the-year bonus check you may have come to expect from your former employer (don't even look for a Christmas turkey). The good news is because there are so few standards on bonuses and perks, you have a better shot at creating a plan for yourself, a plan that delivers exactly what you want. The key thing is to *ask for it*. Be very specific. Do you want a cell phone? A new laptop? More stock options if you achieve certain goals? Relocation assistance if you have to move? These are all in the realm of possibility. Almost everything is negotiable.

---

5. Karl Taro Greenfeld, "Living the Late Shift," *Time*, June 28, 1999, p. 47.
6. Kelly Smith with Robert Kirwan, "America's Best Company Benefits," *Money*, October 1999, p. 126.

There are some key differences between a David and Goliath in this area. A Goliath is more likely to have a predetermined number of options to offer new employees and a limit on bonuses, no matter how well you do. A David will reward you on performance, but what you achieve could be much greater. One note: If you're angling for a bonus or more options, tie them to goals such as achieving certain milestones for the firm. Revenues are a notoriously unreliable benchmark for Web companies.

A David may have a tough time giving you specifics as to what kind of bonuses it can ultimately provide. For now, agree on a ballpark plan with the understanding (in writing) that you'll hammer out specifics later. And remember that no one but you stands to gain from these understandings, so follow up!

Non-monetary perks you can ask for include:

- A new laptop, especially if you're working virtually or will be on the road.

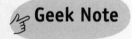 **Geek Note** The rules for exercising options are different for private and public companies. We know of a few people who stayed at a company long enough for their shares to vest, but because the company wasn't yet public, the options were still of highly speculative value. If you depart from such a private company with vested options, you only have a brief window of time to exercise them. That means coming up with cash to buy shares in a company that you've decided not to work for anymore. It's kind of a tough call but may still be worth coughing up the cash for.

▪ Reimbursement for your ISP if you're often expected to log in from home.

▪ A cell phone or two-way pager if you'll be traveling or need to be accessible at any hour.

▪ Vacation: Ask about the policy.

▪ If you'll be attending industry events, they should pay. Establish this early on, so you don't get stuck floating them a loan.

▪ An insurance plan: Many of the larger Internet companies are going above and beyond the call of duty, often paying 100 percent of the plan and covering your entire family. This isn't the case with smaller start-ups. If it doesn't have an insurance plan in place yet, ask the company to pay your COBRA during the gap. It's possible they won't have the same kind of comprehensive coverage a traditional firm offers. You'll have to do the responsible thing yourself.

It may sound silly, but be sure to ask two other key questions:

▪ Where will I sit? (Believe it or not, they may not have thought this one through.)

▪ Is there a computer and a phone available for my use, or do I have to order that? (A good question to ask! When Deborah's new boss told her these things were still to come, she got the chance to custom-order her computer—at company expense.)

A Great Job Title

Although you may not be able to make a convincing case for having "king" or "queen of all the Russias" on your business card, you can usually get a pretty snazzy title from your new Internet boss. This is especially true at a start-up, because they may not have a strong, preconceived idea of your exact responsibilities— and will likely change them anyway! Take the lead on this and create an impressive title for yourself—but, of course, one that has some basis in what you actually *plan* to do.

Virtual Offices and Telecommuting

You put on a pot of coffee and head upstairs to check in with the office via e-mail, still in your flannel bathrobe (this is Cindy's typical morning—although she makes an extra stop to floss). You download some files and start your workday blessedly free of morning traffic reports, crowded trains, or road rage.

If this is your idea of heaven, you'll never have a better opportunity to make it a reality than in the Internet world. After all, these are the guys who invented the technology for telecommuting. *But*—and this is a big *but*—you'll be doing yourself a huge disservice if you start angling for the virtual office too soon. (**Note:** This doesn't apply to community leaders who generally work from home; see chapter 9).

When you're new to a company, any company, there's a lot to learn that you'll never get the hang of unless you're on premises. When you're getting your feet wet in the Web world, there's more than a new corporate culture to reckon with—there's technology and a particular vibe to experience. You can't do that without face time. This is a go-go world; for these ventures to succeed, everyone needs to give it his or her all (this applies to freelancers as well; if you're using the freelance route as a foot in the door, spend as much time as you can on premises during the project to bond with the team).

This exposure to the company is especially important if your job isn't located at the main headquarters. Have them build in orientation and regular visits to HQ for you; it's important to your understanding of the company, as well as your career, that you see and be seen by the key players.

Sure, there are digital workers who are rarely in the office. Among these are programming junkies, customer service reps, and community organizers, but their responsibilities can usually be encapsulated in bullet lists: "monitor this, check that, write code that does this." For the rest of us, the jobs emphasize teamwork. After all, the Web began as a community in which ideas were freely exchanged and everyone's opinion was valued. Even if capitalism has intruded, this spirit of community remains the heart and soul of the Internet world, so be part of it.

And don't forget—the Internet workplace can be just plain fun! With all that creativity and enthusiasm for the Next Big Thing, along with eager twenty-somethings injecting their own skewed energy onto the scene, you're bound to have a pretty good time. It won't look good if you keep that spirit at arms' length.

This doesn't mean you'll *never* be able to work at home. In fact, if it snows, about half of the staff will just take it upon themselves to diligently begin the workday at home. Our advice is to establish yourself at the company before you start asking for an official work-at-home schedule. Once you've proven how valuable you are, you'll be in the driver's seat.

If you've found your dream job and the only thing separating you and it is money, you might be tempted to ask to telecommute as a trade-off. Stifle that thought. You really do need face time when you're just starting out. Instead, try negotiating for a four-day workweek or perhaps early departures two days a week.

Flex Time

When she was still punching in nine to five (more like eight-thirty to six, really), Deborah remembers being grilled by her former boss as to why she was twenty minutes late one morning (it was a doctor's appointment, if you must know). This grade-school tardiness routine drives us both up a wall. Thankfully, it's usually not a big deal in the Internet world, where workplace hours are a lot less regulated (but frequently a lot longer).

The general frenzied pace of the Internet has resulted in an atmosphere where what you *accomplish* is far more important than what time you came in. Thus you may be able to set hours for yourself that are more conducive to your lifestyle. We know one guy who wanders in around noon but works until late at night. Another Internet exec gets in at the crack of dawn, leaves in time for dinner with her family, and then regularly logs in another few hours after the kids' bedtime.

Be smart and take some time to observe the corporate culture to see what's possible for you. You may not need to even ask for flex-time; sometimes it just evolves. One warning though: If you're a clock watcher, the Internet business may not be for you. There's no getting around the fact that hours can be long and unpredictable. If you really need a set routine and it would upset you to get after-hours calls at home, we urge you to think twice—even three times—before going dot-com.

When it comes to perks, keep in mind that you're arriving a

little late to this party and, therefore, are not in the best position to make a lot of demands straightaway. Many of your co-workers quit their jobs three or four years ago to buy into the Internet vision (the really young ones may have never worked in any other business). They're passionate about what they do. They've *earned* the right to work from home, wear silly clothes, or come in at weird hours. If you ask for this or that right from the start, it won't go over well. Take your time, tread lightly, and learn everything you can. Once you've proven that you get it and didn't take the job just so that you could come in to work at noon, you'll have more leverage. Remember that you're making this leap for the long run.

Get It in Writing

Sad but true: The days of the old-fashioned handshake deal are as dead as Jimmy Stewart. Once your boss has verbally agreed to give you what you want, get it in writing.

This is particularly important because of the speed with which things change in the Internet world. What happens if your company is acquired? Or what if this firm's not what you thought it would be and you need to part company? What if your boss leaves right after you start? Here's where a clearly worded, *countersigned* document can make all the difference.

Things that should be spelled out in your employment letter should include:

- Your title and who you report to

- Salary

- When you're up for review and a salary increase

- Number of stock options, their strike price, and when they vest

- Details on any bonus or commission plan, including sign-on. When will they be available—annually? Quarterly? (great if you can swing it); What will it be based on—individual performance? Group achievements?

- Vacation time

- Health plan

- Reimbursement plan for company travel, etc.

- Terms of your employment: You're most likely to be an at-will employee, which means you can resign any time with or without cause. They, in turn, can let you go as well, but should give you a minimum of two weeks' notice. Is there a severance package?

Important: Make sure your vesting options won't be affected by termination; people have been fired the day before their options come due. Add a line in your employment agreement to the effect of "XX firm will exercise the right to terminate in good faith and in any event not in derogation of the employees' right in regard to the vesting stock options" (thanks to our lawyer for that bit of legalese).

Armed with this negotiation know-how, you're primed to make a deal for yourself that takes into account not just your present needs, but the future too (and trust us, it's gonna be a bright one!).

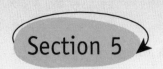

ENJOY THE RIDE

You've survived your last drinking binge with your old work buddies and can hear the rocket boosters warming up on your new Internet career. Strap yourself in, 'cause the blast-off can be a little tricky.

For the rest of the book, consider us mission control, guiding you around the common pitfalls of your transition into this new world. We'll make sure you launch into a safe and secure orbit. Well, as "safe and secure" as the Internet can be, anyway!

Find out:

- What to expect on your first day, first week, first month, and beyond

- What the workplace will be like

- The best ways to make a good impression with your dot-com– savvy co-workers

- How to get noticed by the higher-ups

- Who *not* to ignore on the staff (skip this one at your own peril)

▪ How to survive those first meetings when you have no idea what's going on

And last but not least, we've compiled a list of resources, Web sites, and other tools to help get you through it all. Think of it as a kind of cheat sheet—which, by the way, is available to you in frequently updated form at our Web site, www.notjustgeeks.com (plug, plug). So grab another double latté (you'll learn to love coffee in this world) and push on to the final leg of our journey.

Chapter 16

BECOME AN INTERNET STAR
Thriving in the Dot-Com Universe

At this point, you're probably experiencing a mix of relief ("Whew, I made it through all those interviews!"), excitement ("Sayanora, dead end job!"), and panic ("Omigod, what do I do now????"). Put away the Xanax—we're about to share the pointers to get you over the transition hump, plus a few things we wish someone had told *us*.

Your First Week

Day One. As we've mentioned (constantly), the Internet game is chaotic. It's highly unlikely there will be balloons or any big welcome signs heralding your arrival. In fact, most people won't even know you've been hired—and that includes the receptionist. If you're lucky, someone may have cleared out a space for you to work in—but it's very possible no one's gotten around to it.

Self-sufficiency is the name of the game, kids. Hope that your boss will be around to offer some assistance on the first day (but more likely you'll show up promptly at eight-thirty and he or she will waltz in around eleven). Introduce yourself to the receptionist or whoever answers the phones so you won't miss any calls or visitors. Then get answers to the following questions:

FIRST DAY CHECKLIST

- Where will I sit?

- If there are locks on the door or the desk, do I have keys for them?

- Do I need keys to the office itself? Is there a security system? What is the code?

- Is there a phone? What's my extension?

- How do I get an outside line? Dial nine?

- How do I get voice-mail set-up?

- How do I get my name and extension included in the company voice-mail directory?

- Is there a fax number? What is it?

- Is there a computer in my workspace?

- Is it hooked up to the network already?

- Do I have an e-mail address assigned to me? What is it?

- How do I access my e-mail? What e-mail program do we use here?

- If I'm working remotely, what do I have to do to access my e-mail?

- Do we use instant messaging? If so, which one, and who should I put on my list?

- Is there a companywide directory? How do I get on it?

- How do I order business cards?

- Where's the coffee machine?

- (And most important) Where's the bathroom? Do I need a key?

There may not be a lot of hand-holding during this process, so remember these words: "No whining." You may not know how to set up your own e-mail, but at least turn the computer on and see if it's hooked up to the network. In most cases, the people you'll be asking for help handle this kind of stuff in between their real work, so start off on the right foot by making it as easy and pleasant as possible for them.

When you first started at your old company, some nice HR person probably sent over a thick packet of information about payroll, taxes, and insurance. There might have even been an official orientation, which included lots of filling in of forms. In the busy world of the Internet, if that packet even exists, you'll have to chase it down. Although many Goliath companies *have* taken to orienting new employees, it's still the exception rather than the rule, so make asking for this information one of your first tasks.

Even the youngest start-up will have tax forms and payroll information you'll need to complete. And it's likely that you'll be asked to sign an intellectual property agreement, which means anything you come up with while working for them is theirs. Have a lawyer look it over before you sign it.

The same goes if you're asked to sign an employment agreement with a noncompete clause. They're trying to ensure that you won't work for their competition over a certain period of time, and while that's certainly acceptable during a probationary period, what if you want to leave after only three weeks? If at all possible, don't sign one of these agreements, but if you must, do it after your probationary period is completed and make sure you're only prevented from working for a narrowly defined category of Internet competitors; for example, agreeing not to work for firms in the "family community space" is far less limiting to your future than "all Internet firms."

It would be nice if your boss offers to take you to lunch on your first day, but don't bet on it: It probably won't occur to him or her to take the time out to do this. Try not to get hung up on the social niceties; what you really want is some substantive mind-melding with your new boss within your first few days. Spend some quality time with him or her, and ask them to be very explicit about what is expected from you. Believe it or not, your job description may have changed between the time of your interview and your first day. Did they neglect to mention it?

Ask your boss to spell out your job duties and areas of responsibility. Take lots of notes and ask questions. If your boss talks in shorthand (and many Internet types do), make him or her explain what the heck it means, at least the first time. For instance, if you are asked to contact all of the ISPs in the state, find out whether you are supposed to do a direct-mail piece, send e-mail, pick up the phone, or visit them in person. Does he or she have a list already? Can you buy that list somewhere? If you have to do the research, does he or she have any suggestions? Which decision-maker at the ISP should you reach out to: the president, the director of marketing? You get the drill. Belabor the point until you understand your *boss* and you're both on the same page.

Because there are so few systems or established methods of doing things at dot-coms, personality and style play important roles. It's therefore critical to "know thy boss" and learn what you have to do to make him or her happy.

Take the lead on managing "up," at least as much as you can

without being too obvious. Remember that your boss may be young or not the most experienced manager in the world, so work the relationship to get the guidance you need to get your job done.

Try to establish a set time for checking in with your boss. This could be a daily e-mail update or a fifteen minute sit-down once a week. Find a schedule that works and try to stick to it. This reality check will keep both of you on track. (One caveat: The Internet world is big on self-starters, so don't make this a crutch or become a pain about it.)

Now what about all those other faces buzzing past you in the hall or riding the elevator with you? If you're lucky, someone will walk you around and introduce you, or send an introductory e-mail. Otherwise, take the initiative with anyone who seems open to a friendly approach. It's unlikely you'll work closely with every one of them, but as we've stressed, the digital world is one of big-picture thinking. It's not ghettoized like traditional companies where sales and tech support stick largely to themselves; departments overlap and influence each other in subtle—and not so subtle—ways. One of our sources says that, unlike his former job,

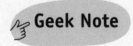 **Geek Note**   It's not at all unusual for management to shift dramatically—and frequently—at Internet companies. The founder may step aside to become a less-available chairman when the company really takes off, for example. *People's* titles and responsibilities shift abruptly and often. What this means to you is that you might have a smart new boss by the time you start, or you could find yourself working for a punk. In the latter case, don't panic; he or she—or you—are likely to move on within the company before too long. And frankly, there's so much work to do, you won't have time to get hung up on whom you report to.

"the people at the highest level regularly interact with people at the lowest level. That's culturally very different, and much more enjoyable."

Start out on the right foot by showing initiative. Get to know what goes on in all the various departments, and meet each team member. Check with your boss and get the okay to set up meetings with the top person in each area. Then let them tell you what they're doing, and introduce you to the folks who work with them.

Don't worry if you're clueless about what it is they do, or how they do it—the great thing about being the newbie in the bunch is that there's never a better time to ask a bunch of dumb questions. Here's your chance to really pick their brains and make them feel important. Not only will you be gaining valuable information, but you'll also be showing respect for their experience and point of view. This can only grease the hinges on your entry into "the club" (just remember, though—there's a fine line between honest curiosity and total sucking up).

Whatever you do, don't overlook those in the tech department. You may have minimal contact with them and think their world is far removed from what you're doing. You may think you don't have to pay them much attention. Wrong! Technology drives the entire Internet economy! These are the people who will put your ideas into action (not to mention fix your computer); it's vitally important that you create a relationship with them. Try to arrange a meeting with the most senior person that you can get a hold of. You'll not only want the nickel tour, you need to know the procedure for getting stuff done. Showing the techies that you understand and respect the importance of their role will make them far more willing to work with you on your brilliant ideas than if you treat them like glorified field hands.

Also pay attention to any staff whom you "inherit." It's likely that they're young, and it's likely that they've been managed badly (or not at all) up to this point. Treat them a bit like you would a skittish animal: Reach out to them, ask them to help you with what you don't know, feed them treats. Build on what they've already done and make sure they know their contributions are valued. They can be the buffer zone between your new (raw) self and upper management, who may not see just how brilliant you are . . . yet. And as much as they can help you, keep in mind that these subordinates can torpedo you quicker than anyone, too. Work hard at maintaining good relationships.

Your First Month

In the early weeks at your new company, get yourself invited to as many meetings as possible. If you hear about one happening that you want to go to, casually ask whose meeting it is, find that person, and ask if you can just quietly sit in. He or she has probably been inviting the same five people to the same weekly meeting for months and just didn't think to include you. Be careful and polite, but try to get in.

Okay, so now you're in that meeting. The jargon's flying and you have no idea what's going on. If possible, wait until after the public gathering to discreetly ask someone what you missed. Don't slow things down by asking for explanations of stuff they all know like the back of their hand. Unless someone point-blank asks you a question, just lay low. You can't be expected to understand everything on Day One (or even Day Ten); they know you don't have Internet experience.

Ask all your dumb questions off-line (meaning, after meetings)—but *ask* them. Trust us, your co-workers will respect you more for owning up to knowledge gaps and doing something about them rather than trying to fake it. We know of one executive, brand-new to the Internet, who didn't understand a key

Web design concept but tried to pretend that she did. It backfired on her—badly—during an important meeting, and her subordinates still make fun of her when she's not around.

Bring associates with you in your early meetings so they can help you find your way through them all until you really know what you're talking about. We can't stress this point enough: *Admit what you don't know*, then learn it.

We've talked about making friends with the obvious players — your boss, department heads—but what about the not-so-obvious ones? At any company, you'll find an underlying power structure. This could include the boss's secretary or the guys in the mailroom who can "accidentally" hold up an important package. The same applies in the Internet world. Take a look around: Who are the go-to guys, the ones who always know the status of every project? Who are the ones leading the after-work beer blasts? Who's the one with all the best gossip in the coffee room? You may not work with them directly, but make no mistake—they influence what it is you're doing (or will want to do in the future). Get to know them, and get on their good side. Deborah remembers working at a company where smokers were banished to an outside terrace. Well, this terrace—which was accessible only if you were willing to climb out of a window—was where all the best buzz was generated. Deborah frequently climbed out that window, even though she doesn't smoke, just to find out what was *really* going on!

By now, you're probably getting the hang of things but perhaps you're still feeling a little left out. We've discussed how important the concept of teamwork is in the Internet business. Don't simply wait for someone to invite you to happy hour or the late-night pizza party—initiate something yourself. Order a six-foot sub for lunch one day, or ask some of your colleagues to join *you* for drinks. You'll be sending a clear signal that you're one of them, or are trying to be. So don't be shy.

This isn't just a good tactic to help you fit in right away—it's groundwork for your future. Virtually everyone at an Internet firm is working something on the side. They are developing cool ideas, have deals going, or are trying to make something happen; it's just a natural offshoot of all the creative juice flowing through the place. The bug will probably bite you at some point. In any case, you never know where your next opportunity will lie, so be on good terms with everyone; the Internet business adds new meaning to the term *networking*.

As you get acquainted with the others, there may be someone who's been around the Virtual Block a time or two. Maybe you share something in common, like you both worked in the same industry before or are both rabid hockey fans. Forge a comfortable relationship. This person would be good to have as an ally, someone who can show you the more informal procedures of the company. (Are memos considered essential to workflow or akin to the plague? Are you "expected" to attend the Friday afternoon recap in the Big Boss's office or is it considered a joke?)

Your ally is the perfect candidate for bouncing ideas off of, especially early in the game. One of the reasons the company hired you is your boundless energy, enthusiasm, and creativity, right? You're probably itching to present about 100 killer ideas and can't wait to hear the words of praise that will undoubtedly be heaped upon you. Whoa, Nellie! Enthusiasm is always welcome in the wired world, but keep in mind the core business of your company. What are the priorities right now? Which of your ideas are really viable? It's times like these that your ally can steer your energy into the most constructive channels and help you avoid looking like too much of a novice. Plus, there's no greater stress-reliever than having someone you can kvetch with over lunch.

From Here to Eternity

Okay, the training wheels are off. You've gotten settled into the daily routine and your adrenaline levels are accustomed to spiking on a regular basis. Now your colleagues will expect you to know what's going on in the business. We hope you're reading the digital newsletters and trade journals we've recommended (see also "Resources"); and remember to notify these publications of your new work e-mail address. You should be more familiar with the jargon, the players, and the info in general and be able to think through what it means to your company. You're no longer dabbling—this is for real.

You now have a clear sense of what your firm is trying to accomplish and the role you play within it. Time to let your ideas and efforts take root—and take off: Let the people around you know what you're up to in a way that makes it clear you understand how it will affect *their* world. This is not just random horntooting; part of the Internet credo is thinking past "your" part and understanding how it fits into the bigger picture (have we stressed this enough yet?). Through a brief e-mail or a casual remark, let people feel that your work is helping them too. Don't

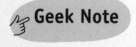 **Geek Note** Pay attention to the stock price of the company if it's public. Yes, it sounds mercenary— but, hey, it's everyone's favorite subject. Bookmark a financial site and check the price occasionally, but not obsessively.

limit your efforts to those people you feel can help you up the ladder—being too exclusive or hoarding information does *not* fly in the digital world. It's about community, remember?

Don't fool yourself into thinking your cool new Internet gig will be free of the stresses of your old job. There are still aggravating issues common to every workplace, plus the added pressure of the industry's take-no-prisoners attitude. There will still be days when you have to choose between your kid's parent-teacher conference and accompanying the president of the company on a cross-country client call. You'll still get out-voted on some things and need to implement plans you disagree with. You'll have to hire or fire people and will probably work harder than you have in a long, long time. The Internet business is a whole lot of fun, but it's not Utopia.

Part of that fun is the result of all the creativity in the air, but part of it is the sheer silliness required to counter the constant pressure. Here are the things that are constantly in the back of everyone's mind.

FUNDING PRESSURES

How much money do we have and how quickly are we burning through it? Do we need to go for another round? How much do we need to ask for, and to whom will we go to this time? Is it time to go IPO? Or should we sell or combine our company with another? How do we make that happen, and who does the negotiation? Yadda, yadda, yadda.

COMPETITIVE ARENA

Nowhere are you more visible to your competitors than on the Internet. What are our competitors doing better than we are and how can we surpass them as quickly as possible? Does the market perceive them as better than us?

ALWAYS ON

An Internet company never has a day off. If the Web site goes down over Memorial Day weekend, someone has to fix it. E-commerce sites sell stuff twenty-four hours a day and need customer-service staff to match those hours. It never, ever lets up. That's part of the addictive buzz, but it also ratchets up the exhaustion factor.

CORPORATE CULTURE

If the copy machine runs out of paper, don't wait for some imaginary assistant to handle it—do it yourself. The same goes if someone left empty pizza boxes in the conference room. Being a trouper is one of those intangible qualities that can do more for your success in the wired world than knowledge of the latest programming tool.

We've said this a few times already, but it's worth repeating: You're a little bit late to the party, so don't pull an attitude around those who got into this game before you (conversely, don't react to any attitude you may encounter from them). Early Internet types have a true passion—it keeps them going during the late nights and jitters about their financial future. To them, you're something of an interloper who's just now joining after they tackled the scariest, hardest parts. This certainly doesn't mean they'll never like or respect you; just remember your place in the food chain for now. They'll soon discover how valuable you are to the team.

And they'll spot *your* passion for their business before long. After all, something compelled you to buy this book (especially because you're not related to either of us). You obviously have a desire to do more with your career, to stretch, to grow, to take a few chances. You want to come off of the sidelines and get into the game. That kind of enthusiasm will carry you a long, long way in your new Internet career.

We've downloaded just about everything we could think of to make the transition fairly painless and set you up for success. It all comes from hard-earned experience, but you may have some helpful insights of your own before long—in which case, please share your stories with us (along with others preparing to pole vault into the digital world) at http://www.notjustgeeks.com.

Okay, if we could distill the entire contents of this book into a cheat sheet you could carry with you in your head, here are the most important things to remember on your journey:

- Know what's happening in the industry in general and your category in particular.

- Keep learning everything you can.

- Embrace the technology.

- Don't be afraid to ask questions.

- Think outside the box.

But, of course, the most important key to enjoying a blazingly successful Internet career is to have some fun while you're doing it. No matter how harried you may feel, or how behind schedule a project is, remember to lighten up and treat this like the great adventure it is. This is an exciting time to be in the work world, a time of groundbreaking change. And you're about to become part of it. Welcome to the new frontier!

RESOURCES

The following pages contain resources we've personally found useful for getting—and staying—up to speed about the ever-changing Internet business world. Included are fifty high-rated Web sites, as determined by Jupiter Media Metrix (www.mediametrix.com). These change monthly (sometimes even hourly), but we thought it would provide a good jumping off point for you.

Remember these are general resources; don't forget to go back to the specialty chapters for Internet organizations, etc., specific to your industry.

Naturally, in the fast-paced world of the Internet, information constantly changes, so we strongly encourage you to visit our Web site, www.notjustgeeks.com, for current updates.

Happy hunting!

Web Sites for General Internet Information

http://www.internetnews.com
Front-page news.

http://www.zdnet.com/intweek
Interactive Week magazine's online site, produced by parent Ziff Davis, ZD net; lots of links, kind of tech-heavy.

http://www.herring.com
  Red Herring magazine's online site. Good list of industry events; good investor information.

http://www.internet.com
  Basic industry information on the front page.

http://www.webopedia.com
  Dictionary of definitions; good general resource.

http://www.seminars.internet.com
  List of upcoming industry seminars in various areas.

http://events.internet.com
  List of events from Internet World (produced by Penton Media, these are the big trade shows). Find out when/where the next one is and go.

http://cyberatlas.internet.com
  Good reference information on the industry, top Web site lists, industry analysis. Has the best demographics, basic industry info, plus specialized coverage (online financial, etc.).

http://www.iconocast.com
  One of our favorites: great industry analysis, inside gossip (sometimes so "inside" that no one but the guy who writes it understands it!). His weekly newsletter is a must-read.

http://www.vault.com
  Has message boards about many of the bigger Internet companies. Don't believe everything you read, but it might be a way to find an insider to provide you with info before an interview.

http://www.thestandard.com
  Great general site.

http://www.fastcompany.com
  Online version of a good magazine; the career/working section has some great articles in the archives.

http://www.jup.com

Jupiter Media Metrix Communications Web site. They're a major research firm and post interesting articles, plus information about seminars and trade shows.

http://www.forrester.com

Another big Internet research firm, with interesting snippets from reports and studies plus info on seminars.

http://www.gartner.com

Another research company, this one more specialized in technology and IT consulting, but also has more broadly based seminars and research reports.

http://www.business2.com

The online site of *Business 2.0* magazine.

http://www.news.com

CNet site; covers the industry as a whole. Not quite as specialized as some of the other resources.

http://www.individual.com

Covers different industries, with highlights on the Internet business.

http://www.mediametrix.com

This is the biggest rating company. Lists of top sites, plus news about Internet traffic and trends.

http://www.next20years.com

Runs seminars about the digital future. Good exhibits and shmooze opportunities.

http://www.cbsmarketwatch.com

Good industry coverage, must-read daily Internet newsletter.

http://www.wired.com

Wired magazine online, the granddaddy of them all. We like the calendar of "e-vents" and the "Current Hoo Ha" (what people are talking about).

http://www.davenetics.com

Written by a crazy guy named Dave Pell. He calls himself a "dot-conomist" and sends out a daily newsletter with info compiled from many different sources. A good spin on the Internet biz; good reading for all.

http://www.upside.com

Upside daily tech news, associated with *Upside* magazine. Has a daily Upside Direct newsletter. Their "Elite 100" lists the movers and shakers in the business.

http://www.ditherati.com

Quotes of the day chosen by deep industry insiders. Fun, but maybe not all that relevant—except if you want to feel hip.

http://www.internetwire.com

Features various sections devoted to different industries. Good for those looking to transition to the Internet, since it covers wired and unwired news of industries.

http://www.andovernews.com

Good coverage of general tech stuff.

http://www.bizjournals.com/

Consortium of business magazines for various cities around the country. Great resource for finding local Internet businesses and uncovering job opportunities.

http://www.recruitersnetwork.com/

An online site devoted to online recruiters! Even has a daily recruiting newsletter.

http://www.hr-guide.com/

Pretty good list of resources, documents, etc., for recruiting, human resources in general.

http://www.winm.org

Women in New Media group. Has good lunches/seminars in New York. You're supposed to be "recommended" to join. Beg your way into the first function, then go network like crazy.

http://ecompany.com
   Digital version of the magazine covering the new economy.

http://www.industryscoop.com
   Semi-monthly electronic newsletter covering technology, tools, products, and services.

http://www.businessjeeves.com
   Good directory of business sites.

http://www.iab.net/events/eventsource.html
   Good list—by category—of various industry events.

http://www.ad-guide.com/
   Good lists of resources, including Web marketing firms and event listings.

http://www.nytimes.com
   Cybertimes and Circuits sections online. Good specialty areas on entertainment, arts, education, cyberlaw, etc.

REGIONAL

http://www.alleyevents.com
   Comprehensive listing of NYC new media industry events and links.

http://www.atnewyork.com
   Good market intelligence on the industry, particularly NY-based companies. Has a great newsletter everyone should subscribe to, no matter where they live.

http://www.nynma.org
   The New York New Media Association. Has terrific jobs board and lists all the events worth knowing about in NYC.

http://www.norcalcompanies.com
   Directory of companies in Northern California. Good resource for finding the basic info on firms; you have to pay to get more detailed information.

http://www.bayarea.com
The *San Jose Mercury News* is the local newspaper for Silicon Valley. This site covers news on companies and activities there.

http://www.siliconvalleycareers.com/
Good spot to find out all about California-based high-tech employers.

http://www.siliconalleydaily.com
Inside dope on NY-area stuff.

http://www.craigslist.org
Community boards for many cities.

☞ OUR LIST OF GREAT JOB SITES

Web sites come and go, and who's to say these will still be up by the time you read this! But they're hot enough to stand a pretty good chance!

http://www.monster.com
http://www.jobsonline.com
http://www.headhunter.net
http://www.careerbuilder.com
http://www.hotjobs.com
http://www.wetfeet.com
http://www.cruelworld.com
http://www.guru.com
http://www.freeagent.com
http://www.flipdog.com
http://www.6figurejobs.com
http://www.jobsonline.com

Trade Magazines

You may already be reading some of these print publications; if not, pay a visit to your local newsstand . . . NOW! Many of these also offer online versions (mentioned above).

Fast Company

Business 2.0

The Industry Standard

Internet World

Red Herring

Advertising Age

Business Week

Entrepreneur

Wired

Inter@ctive Week

Revolution

eCompany Now

Richard's Essential Reading List

Richard Laermer of RLM Public Relations, one of the hottest Internet PR firms going, was nice enough to share the same must-read list he gives his new hires, along with his comments on his recommendations. Thanks, Richard!

NEWSPAPERS

The New York Times: A separate consumer technology section called "Circuits" comes out on Thursdays.

The Wall Street Journal: Watching the Web, a column that highlights new and interesting Web sites, appears fortnightly on Thursdays. Main technology coverage is on Thursdays (check out Walter Mossberg's column).

USA Today: Tech Extra section appears on Wednesdays.

E-MAILS

@NY: Daily e-mail top-notch news and analysis. Associated Web site is http://www.atnewyork.com.

Silicon Alley Daily: News of the day. Associated monthly magazine is *Silicon Alley Reporter* (http://www.siliconalleyreporter.com). Notorious for its claim as the true, original voice of the Alley. Hmmm . . .

Industry Standard Media Grok (http://www.industrystandard.com): Daily e-mail with handy roundup of mainstream media coverage of current tech-industry news stories. Very entertaining and useful for getting to know all of the other major reporters, especially ntheir beats and specialties. Written by the @NY people.

Seidman's Online Insider: Robert Seidman writes how he wants about what he wants, which includes glimpses into the life of a tech-nerd. Emphasis is on broadband technology, pet peeves, and protagonists. AOL is one of the causes he champions.

The CyberScene (http://www.cyberscene.com): Gossipy Friday e-mail from Courtney Pulitzer, who rounds up the parties of the week.

VentureWire: National roundup of significant investments in technologies companies. Published by Technologic Partners.

ONLINE PUBLICATIONS

News.com: CNet's daily news feed. Features coverage of several key sectors of the technology industry. The place to be featured online.

Internet.com

CMP/TechWeb: Business news online with a technical slant.

ZDNet.com

Wired News: Handy, but not as broad in scope nor indispensable as *News.com.*

We've already listed some of Richard's must-read publications above in "Trade Magazines." He also recommends the following:

INTERNET/IT PUBLICATIONS

Release 1.0: The most theoretical and intellectual of technical publications about the new business economy. $700 a year to subscribe, but you should know about it. Written by Esther Dyson and Kevin Werbach, both big players.

BUSINESS PUBLICATIONS

Crain's NY: Weekly New York–oriented business publication with healthy amounts of tech coverage. Other *Crain's* are published in Chicago and Detroit among other places.

Forbes: Print and Web versions.

Business Week: Print magazine.

Brill's Content: Print. Steve Brill dissects the media that analyzes the world with often-hilarious results.

ADVERTISING PUBLICATIONS
Internet Advertising Report: Daily e-mail newsletter.

AdWeek: Print and online versions.

Sales & Marketing Management: Print. Hey, there's a world outside new media.

TELEVISION
CNN: *Digital Jam*
        Entrepreneurs Only
        Squawk Box

CNBC: *Power Lunch*

The Top 50 Web Sites[a]

The Internet business is constantly in transition; by the time you read this, the picture may have changed dramatically for the following firms. However, we list them here to give you a little bit of a snapshot of the business as a whole.

Since many of these companies are continually buying other firms or Web sites, visit their site for the most current, detailed information about what their company is up to (this week!), and job opportunities not only with them, but also with their new acquisitions.

We've listed the city where their corporate headquarters are located; if it's nowhere near where you live, don't let that stop

---

[a]Per MediaMetrix.com, February 2000.

you. You'll often find possibilities outside the headquarter city, including international.

1. AOL Network (http://www.aol.com)
What It Does: ISP, content, and community.
Headquarters: Dulles, VA.

2. Yahoo.com (http://www.yahoo.com)
What It Does: Search engine.
Headquarters: Santa Clara, CA.

3. Microsoft Sites (http://www.microsoft.com)
What It Does: Software and more.
Headquarters: Redmond, WA.

4. Lycos (http://www.lycos.com)
What It Does: Search engine.
Headquarters: Waltham, MA (offices also in New York, L.A., San Francisco, Miami, Chicago, Dallas, and Pittsburgh).

5. Excite @Home (http://www.excite.com)
What It Does: Search engine and portal and ISP.
Headquarters: Redwood City, CA.

6. Go Network (http://www.go.com)
What It Does: Search engine and portal.
Headquarters: Sunnyvale, CA, and Seattle, WA.

7. NBC Internet (http://www.nbci.com)
What It Does: The interactive division of NBC; includes search engines like Snap, plus entertainment content.
Headquarters: San Francisco, CA, and New York, NY.

8. Amazon.com (http://www.amazon.com)

What It Does: e-commerce site specializing in books, music.
Headquarters: Seattle, WA.

9. Time Warner (http://www.timewarner.com)
What It Does: Parent company of properties including Pathfinder, CNN.com, Turner Broadcasting, and about a gazillion others.
Headquarters: New York, NY.

10. About.com (http://www.about.com)
What It Does: Provides information and links to various topics via expert "guides."
Headquarters: New York, NY.

11. Go2Net.com (http://www.go2net.com)
What It Does: Watch this site, recently merged with Info Space.
Headquarters: Seattle, WA.

12. Real.com (http://www.real.com)
What It Does: Provides music and video software via streaming media.
Headquarters: Seattle, WA.

13. AltaVista (http://www.altavista.com)
What It Does: Search engine.
Headquarters: Palo Alto, CA.

14. EBay (http://www.ebay.com)
What It Does: Online auction site.
Headquarters: San Jose, CA.

15. AskJeeves (http://www.askjeeves.com)
What It Does: Search engine.
Headquarters: Emeryville, CA.

16. LookSmart (http://www.looksmart.com)
What It Does: Search engine.
Headquarters: San Francisco, CA.

17. ZDNet (http://www.zdnet.com)
What It Does: Tech site with downloads and market info from Ziff Davis.
Headquarters: New York, NY.

18. CNet.com (http://www.cnet.com)
What It Does: Computer and technology content.
Headquarters: San Francisco, CA.

19. Juno.com (http://www.juno.com)
What It Does: ISP.
Headquarters: New York, NY, and Boston, MA.

20. Infospace.com (http://www.infospace.com)
What It Does: Directory
Headquarters: Redmond, WA.

21. Viacom (http://www.viacom.com)
What It Does: Parent company for MTV sites (includes MTV and VH-1).
Headquarters: New York, NY.

22. The Weather Channel (http://www.weather.com)
What It Does: Weather information.
Headquarters: Atlanta, GA.

23. GoTo.com (http://www.goto.com)
What It Does: Search engine.
Headquarters: Pasadena, CA.

24. AT&T (http://www.att.com)

What It Does: ISP wireless content.
Headquarters: New York, NY.

25. AmericanGreetings (http://www.americangreetings.com)
What It Does: Online greeting cards.
Headquarters: Cleveland, OH.

26. CitySearch-TicketMaster Online (http://www.citysearch.com)
What It Does: Local and regional entertainment directory/
search engine.
Headquarters: Pasadena, CA.

27. IWon (http://www.iwon.com)
What It Does: Prize-oriented portal site.
Headquarters: Irvington, NY.

28. eUniverse Network (http://www.euniverse.com)
What It Does: Youth-oriented game content.
Headquarters: Wallingford, CT.

29. Snowball (http://www.snowball.com)
What It Does: Various content for "Internet generation."
Headquarters: San Francisco, CA, and New York, NY.

30. SmartBotPro (http://www.smartbotpro.net)
What It Does: Bluntly put, a junk e-mail program overseen by
the notorious King of Spam, Sanford Wallace.
Headquarters: Philadelphia, PA (we think—he keeps a low profile for obvious reasons).

31. iVillage.com: The Women's Network (http://www.ivillage.
com)
What It Does: Content and community for women.
Headquarters: New York, NY.

32. CDNow.com (http://www.cdnow.com)
What It Does: Music content and e-commerce.

Headquarters: Ft. Washington, PA.

33. FortuneCity (http://www.fortunecity.com)
What It Does: Community and content.
Headquarters: New York, NY.

34. Macromedia (http://www.macromedia.com)
What It Does: Internet products and technology like Flash and Shockwave.
Headquarters: San Francisco, CA.

35. FreeLotto (http://www.freelotto.com)
What It Does: Sweepstakes and gaming site.
Headquarters: Montreal.

36. Earthlink (http://www.earthlink.net)
What It Does: ISP.
Headquarters: Atlanta, GA (with several offices throughout the United States).

37. BarnesandNoble (http://www.bn.com)
What It Does: The online version of the national book chain.
Headquarters: New York, NY.

38. The Women.com Networks (http://www.women.com)
What It Does: Content and community for women.
Headquarters: San Mateo, CA.

39. Travelocity (http://www.travelocity.com)
What It Does: Travel site.
Headquarters: Ft. Worth, TX.

40. OnHealth (http://www.onhealth.com)
What It Does: Health-related content and services, now associated with WebMD.
Headquarters: Seattle, WA.

41. MarketWatch (http://www.marketwatch.com)
What It Does: Financial information.
Headquarters: New York, NY.

42. MyPoints (http://www.mypoints.com)
What It Does: Direct-marketing service for the Internet, based on incentive points.
Headquarters: New York, NY.

43. TheGlobe (http://www.theglobe.com)
What It Does: Community site.
Headquarters: New York, NY (with offices throughout the United States).

44. Bonzi (http://www.bonzi.com)
What It Does: Software. Now part of NBCi.
Headquarters: San Luis Obispo, CA.

45. Uproar (http://www.uproar.com)
What It Does: Games and entertainment.
Headquarters: New York, NY.

46. LifeMinders (http://www.lifeminders.com)
What It Does: Content and e-mail services to help members "manage" their lives more effectively.
Headquarters: Herndon, VA.

47. MapQuest (http://www.mapquest.com)
What It Does: Driving directions, traffic info, etc. Now owned by AOL.
Headquarters: Denver, CO.

48. News Corp. (http://www.newscorp.com)
What It Does: Interactive divisions of News Corp.'s many businesses, which include Fox TV, *TV Guide* magazine, 20th

Century Fox films, and more.
Headquarters: New York, NY.

49. Sony Online (http://www.sony.com)
What It Does: The entertainment and technology giant.
Headquarters: New York, NY.

50. Quicken (http://www.quicken.com)
What It Does: The financial service software site; features finance-related content.
Headquarters: Mountain View, CA.

As you will see, these sites change frequently! Stay up to date with the most recent top fifty at http://www.mediametrix.com.